Box 175

Inspired by True Love Letters

by

Pebble Day

Box 175 *Inspired by True Love Letters*

ISBN (9781952129001)
Printed in USA. Honeycomb Publishing

Dedication

This book has been a joy to bring to life. For years we have participated in the hearing and telling of our parents' and grandparents' enduring love. We are so proud to be products of their legacy. They come from a lost era of emotional vulnerability and open affection.

Their journey towards one another is highlighted through the forgotten art of letter writing. Their worn and carefully preserved bundles of letters, written in each of their own eloquent hands, are treasured by our family.

Their unabashed loyalty and care for each other reminds us of the beauty to be found within genuine human relationship. We dedicate this book to Henry and Opal for teaching us that commitment is where true romance begins.

Forever yours,

Pam, Heather and Holly

Table of Contents

Chapter One

January 15, 1928
San Pedro, CA

~~Dear Opal.~~ ~~Dearest Opal.~~ My sweet, Opal Pleasant,

I am writing to you because I feel badly about how we left things. How I left things. I know you were angry with me for many reasons, ~~one of which being my leaving to California to look for work~~. I wish things didn't have to be this way. I wish we could still be together.

I love you Opal

The paper taunted me as I sat at the kitchen table, trying to think of the right words to say to her. I scratched out line after line, hoping to beget some brilliantly crafted letter that could win her back. Nothing. Nothing came to mind, and I knew that nothing was going to. It was clear that Opal and I were done. How could we possibly make things work when we were halfway across the country from each other?

I thought about my hometown. I thought about St. Louis and all the people I had left behind. I remembered Mrs. Cartwright, the old woman who used to knit quilts for the orphanage in her spare time. She got so quick with her hands that she was donating about two quilts a week. I thought about Dr. Sherman, the town doctor, who raced over to my home on New Year's Eve three years ago when my father suddenly took ill. But mostly, I thought about Opal. Her presence could light up a room, and it consumed me every time I was near her. To think that we might not ever see each other again was not only heartbreaking; it was terrifying. What kind of man will I be without her? I knew she would never forgive me. She already hadn't. The New Year's Eve party at her best friend Laura's place was proof enough; she hardly spoke to me at all.

My memories carried me back to six months ago, back to the first mistake - being in the wrong place at the wrong time. I still remember the day like it was yesterday. I was at the drugstore picking up my father's prescription when a gentleman walked in. He wore a navy, Ivy League suit, tailored perfectly, right down to the cuffs. He walked right up to the counter and rung the small bell. A clerk from the back walked out with a smile.

"May I help you?" the clerk asked.

"Yes, I need something for an upset stomach. My mother's been in bed all morning, and I'll need her well by sun-up tomorrow," said the well-dressed gentleman.

"Of course. Let me see what I can find," the clerk said with a chipper smile. He stepped away from the counter and led the nicely dressed man down an aisle. I walked up to the counter and waited. Before long, the clerk returned to his place behind the counter.

"What can I help you with today, Sir?" he said.

"I'm here to pick up a prescription for my father. The name should be under Viefhaus," I replied.

"Yes, we just filled his prescription this morning," the clerk said, grabbing a bottle from a neatly organized group behind him. "That'll just be fifteen cents."

"Fifteen cents?" I asked, my pride sinking lower into my chest as I gripped the dime in my pocket. "I was sure his prescription was ten cents."

"That was for the old prescription," the clerk proclaimed with a sigh. "It looks like the doctor changed the medicine to something a little stronger. This one's fifteen cents."

"I'm sorry. I only brought ten with me," I announced with shame.

"I think I've got five cents to spare," I heard a voice from behind me say. I turned to see the nicely dressed gentleman digging through his pockets and quickly producing a nickel. The last of my pride seemed to wither away as I had no choice but to accept the man's kind offer.

"Thank you," I said with a curt smile. "If you give me your address, I'll be sure to mail that back to you just as soon as I'm home."

"Don't bother. I found it outside on my way in anyway," he said with a wink. I laughed and felt my shoulders relax again. I handed the clerk the nickel along with my dime and grabbed my father's prescription.

"Thanks again, mister. I'm sorry. I didn't get your name," I said, extending my hand towards him.

"Jeffrey Warlow, and your name?" he asked, with a firm handshake.

"Henry Viefhaus. And might I add, that's a fine suit. You pick that up at Ashworth's?"

"Actually, I don't live locally. I'm just in town for a wedding. I'm rooted in California," Jeffrey announced with a bashful smile.

"Wow, California? I've got a brother there. I heard it's expensive out that way," I admitted, wondering to myself how anyone was making a decent living in such an overpriced place.

"You'd think, but the jobs match the prices," he said with a confidence I was instantly jealous of. "I actually bought this suit with a bonus."

"No kidding," I replied, giving the tailored suit another envious glance.

"I don't know what your situation is, but I'm the head of the printing department at a newspaper company in Los Angeles," Jeffrey boasted, pulling a business card from his inner jacket pocket. "I've got a few openings if you're interested. Perhaps we could talk business sometime."

At that moment, I thought about my list of to-dos for the day. I had to bring my father back his prescription. I had to pick up Opal and then head down to a New Year's party that I knew I'd get roped into helping set up and tear down. I was about to say no when in walked Thomas Laverne, the thorn in my side.

"Henry! Good to see you," he said, walking right up to the counter.

"Good day, Thomas," I replied through gritted teeth.

"I need twelve pints of ipecac syrup. Flu season has begun, and I'm making house calls by the dozen," Thomas proclaimed to the clerk, pulling out a ten-dollar bill.

"So, Henry, how's that Opal doing?" Thomas prodded, collecting his leftover change.

My blood turned hot the minute he said her name. Thomas Laverne had been trying to steal Opal from me since the minute I laid eyes on her. He was apprenticing under Doctor Sherman and was said to soon be starting his own practice.

"I was headed down to her house now. I bought her a necklace from Morgan's Jeweler, and I was so excited that I decided to deliver the gift in person. I can't wait to see the look on her face. I'll bet she's never seen a real diamond. Am I right?" he said, nudging me with a laugh.

The hairs on the back of my neck stood at attention. Thomas knew my one flaw, and it killed me. Without another second to think, I turned back toward Jeffrey with grateful eyes.

"Got any time right now?" I asked, practically sweating with desperation.

"I like your urgency," Jeffrey says, smiling.

Yes, that was the day that changed everything. From that moment on, I've been trying desperately to put my life back together. I just had to get Opal to forgive me.

I sat at my kitchen table and allowed my mind to wander off to a place where Opal and I could one day be together. It was wishful thinking, but she was the only person I could ever imagine myself being with. I took one final glance at the letter I had been working on before crumpling it and tossing it in the trash bin. If I can't have her, then I'd guess God has destined me to be alone.

Chapter Two

4 Months Later
Henry

"If we're going to make it in time, we'd better not stop at the post office," Dottie said, pulling her coat around her tight to protect herself from the cold. I smiled at her as we strolled down the sidewalk. She was digging through her purse, looking for a lighter. If she wasn't chewing a piece of gum, she was pressing a cigarette to her lips. A blonde curl fell against her cheek as she hung her head low, burying her face in her purse to find a light. She was a sweet little thing and pretty too. When I was with her, I hardly thought about anything or anyone — not even Opal.

"What, are you in some kinda rush to get to work on time? Jeffrey lets you do whatever you please. You practically run Edmunds and Company," I said, nudging her. Dottie hinted a coy smile at me as she lit her cigarette, pretending not to notice my comment. "C'mon, I have to check for a package I'm expecting from my father. It should be here any day now," I said, still heading towards the post office entrance.

"Oh, alright, Henry. But if we're even a minute late, it's your desk I'll be pointing out to Jeffrey," Dottie declared confidently.

"That's if you can get him away from yours," I replied with a smirk.

Dottie rolled her eyes and scolded me as she giggled. "Mr. Viefhaus, I haven't the slightest idea what you're referring to, and if you don't quit this instant, I'll be forced to find a new partner to ride the bus with." She laughed and hit my shoulder playfully. We both had a laugh. It felt good to laugh.

"Alright, alright. I'll behave," I chuckled. Dottie patted my shoulder and clung to my arm as we walked. The post office was just at the end of the block. I knew because I could hear the chatter from the barbershop next door.

"It's 8:15. Better hurry if we want to make the 8:30 bus," Dottie said, more anxiously this time. We picked up the pace as we approached the post office, almost out of breath. I quickly ran in with Dottie following behind me. I walked over to the booth where old Milford was perched with his glasses seated at the tip of his nose.

"Well, look who it is! Henry, good to see you," Milford beamed. He was a chubby old man. Milford grew one of those fancy mustaches that curled at the tips and was completely white on account of his age. "I suppose you're here to check on that package you been waiting on from St. Louis?"

"Yes, Sir. Has it arrived? My Pa said it should be in no later than Friday." Milford turned his back to me as he hobbled into the backroom to check. I tapped my fingers impatiently on the countertop as I waited.

"What're you so anxious about? You feelin' alright?" I glanced over at Dottie only to notice that as she was applying a fresh coat of lipstick. She was staring at my hands with a concerned expression. I quit my fidgeting and looked back at the door to the backroom. Milford still wasn't back yet.

"Oh, I'm alright. Just haven't heard much from my family since I left St. Louis is all," I said to throw her off. She gave me a sorrowful look but chose not to pry. She went back to applying her lipstick just as Milford burst through the door with a little brown box in his hands.

“Here we are!” He set the small box down on the counter and squinted his eyes at the fine print on the address label. “Ah, Mr. Henry Viefhaus. That’s you! I’ll need a quick signature in our log to show that you received it.” I quickly signed for it and grabbed the box from atop the counter.

“Thank you, Milford. You have a pleasant day,” I said with a wave. Milford nodded as Dottie stood by the window and tapped her foot. I hugged the little brown box under my arm and paced over to her. She linked arms with me as we stepped outside. The sun was already bright and warming up the sidewalk as we strolled briskly.

“So, what’s in the box?” Dottie grazed her slim fingers against the hollow cardboard as her red fingernail polish caught my eye. “Your daddy send you somethin’ special?” I didn’t want to tell her what was inside. It was too personal. I knew she would poke fun at me; she had a witty sense of humor. I shook my head at her and gave her a polite grin. Her smile faded to a frown. I could tell she was a little taken back by the fact that, for once, I was managing to keep something confidential. “Oh, c’mon, Hank. You couldn’t possibly keep a secret from lil’ ol’ me?”

“Mr. Viefhaus! Just a moment there, Sir.” Dottie and I turned to see Milford hobbling down the street corner to catch us before we crossed. I paced back to meet him, so he wouldn’t have to walk so far on his bad leg. “Whew! I’m glad I caught you before you crossed.”

“Is everything alright, Milford?” I put my hand on his shoulder to steady him as he tried to catch his breath. He nodded his head and handed me an envelope as he spoke through jagged breaths.

“I forgot to give you this letter that came for you last week. It looks like it may have gotten lost on its way here. It’s dated back from March.” I looked at the envelope, and as I read it, my heart froze. The first words I saw were “Opal Pleasant, St. Louis, Missouri.” “I sure hope that letter wasn’t on a deadline or nothin’ serious, but I suppose mail operations can be funny like that sometimes.” Milford babbled on as I tried to collect myself in front of Dottie.

“Thank you, Milford. We’d best be going now.” He nodded kindly and turned back towards the post office. Dottie leaned over my shoulder to get a look at the letter. I quickly pocketed the envelope inside my coat; I didn't want her trying to make me open it in front of her.

"Who's the letter from? You got a pen pal or somethin'?" I shook my head at her but kept quiet. I couldn't speak. My mind was racing a million miles per second. What could Opal have written? I wanted to hope for the best. I wanted to expect that my dear sweet Opal would say that she forgave me and was ready to take me back. But deep down, I feared the worst. I knew no kind words could come from this letter, especially seeing as how I messed things up with her so badly.

Dottie rolled her eyes, no longer interested in my lost-in-thought routine. "Mr. Viefhaus has two secrets. Whaddya know. You're two for two Henry." She gave me a sarcastic grin as she reached in her purse and pulled out another cigarette. I could tell my silence had sullied her mood. I tried to perk up as much as I could.

"So, any plans for the weekend? I heard Jeffrey might be taking you out on the town Saturday night. Is that true?" Her dour glance was more than enough to get the hint.

"Well, this is the first I'm hearing of it. He can't just take me to God knows where at the drop of a dime. He hasn't even asked me! Sometimes men get me so angry. I just wanna spit."

"Alright, Dottie, now just calm down. I didn't mean to upset you." She managed to give a polite grin, but she was not amused. "And you know, for what it's worth, I think Jeffrey's a fine fellow. What's wrong with him being a little smitten?"

Dottie took a drag from her cigarette and puffed out a smoke cloud as she rolled her eyes. "Oh, just drop it. You wouldn't understand." I chuckled nervously as we approached the bus stop.

The bus ride was filled with people all trudging off to work for the last day of the week. It felt good to know I would have two whole days to myself to do absolutely nothing if I pleased. We rode the *315* bus all the way into Carson before switching to the *87* that would take us the rest of the way into Los Angeles. Once aboard the second bus, it seemed the dust had finally settled as people went back to reading their papers.

Dottie focused her eyes on the *Los Angeles Daily Times* while I thought about that letter from Opal. It was burning a hole through my pocket, but seeing as how we left things before, I dared not open it now.

When we arrived at the office, the day had already begun. Secretaries were typing as fast as their fingers could catch up. I could see Jeffrey in his back office. He had his feet propped on top of his desk and was staring through his office windows out onto the floor. Dottie caught his glance and immediately excused herself. "I'm flushed, Henry dear. I'm going to go freshen up." She handed me her purse and coat. "Would you be a doll and put my things down at my desk?" I nodded as she swiftly escaped just as Jeffrey came prowling from his office to approach us.

"Morning, Henry," Jeffrey said, disappointed. I nodded and removed my hat. "Where'd Dottie run off to? I wanted to ask her something." He slicked down his hair as he cackled aloud and gave me a wink as if I was supposed to understand his predator-like mannerisms. I could see now why Dottie wasn't interested. Jeffrey just wasn't an enjoyable man. He had a distasteful, cavalier way about him, especially when it came to women. He was always treading through the office, preying on the reluctant few that worked with us. Any woman could sense his claws from a mile away.

"I think she excused herself to the ladies' room."
Jeffrey nodded and gave me his best fake smile. I hated that I had a boss that was a whole year younger than me; it just wasn't natural. I gave a final nod and headed off towards my desk.

"Oh, and Henry, one more thing." I turned with just the last bit of nerve I had left for this adventurous morning. "I don't want you forgetting that this is our busy season. No distractions, understood?" I nodded, wondering why he felt the need to tell me that. "I'm gonna need forty-five full copies of the projection notes for next quarter typed up and on my desk before you leave." My expression must've said it all; I hated being a desk clerk. I also knew that Jeffrey picked on me on account of my being the new hire in the office. He was always giving me more work than the others. "It's for the meeting we have on Monday with Edison. All of their executives are going to be needing a copy, so make sure they're clean. No mistakes." His voice was stern like he was my father giving me a lecture on good typing skills. I nodded curtly and bowed out to my desk, dropping off Dottie's things along the way.

The longer I sat there at my desk, the more terrifying the letter in my pocket became. I retrieved the smooth envelope from my jacket and reread the name. Opal Pleasant. It was dated March 21st. I looked at my calendar in the top right corner of my desk. It was May 18th. Almost two whole months had gone by. I placed the letter down on the desk and let it torture me for a while. I made up my mind right then that I would read it when I got home tonight. I didn't have time to be distracted, and Opal would definitely pose a distraction. Jeffrey walked over with a stack of papers clutched tightly in his hands.

"Mr. Viefhaus, I don't want to have to remind you again that your time is of the essence today." He slammed the papers down on the desk, covering Opal's letter in the commotion. "Get to work."

"Yes, Sir. Sorry, Sir," I said, reluctantly sifting through the stack. Jeffrey trotted away, leaving me with a mound of papers to sort through. I dove straight into the pile, and soon my desk was covered in notes for next week's meeting. I quickly forgot about Opal's letter as I stressed to get all the work done before closing time. A few hours later, Dottie was strolling over to my desk with a sweet grin.

"Henry dear, have you had any supper?" I looked up confused and in a daze as I did a glance around the office. Everyone had left.

"Supper? You mean lunch?" She shook her head and smiled at me as she perched herself at the edge of my desk.

"No. You missed lunch." She held her wrist out to show me her watch. "It's 5:30. Are you going to stay for a while?" I couldn't believe where the time had gone. I had been stuck trying to finish all the work for Jeffrey. I wound up working without ceasing throughout the entire day. I rubbed my temples and sat up straight.

"No, no, I'll be right there." I wasn't nearly finished with my workload for the day, but I knew I needed to get some rest. I was also eager to get home and read Opal's letter. I picked up the whole stack of papers assuming it would reveal Opal's letter. To my surprise, the letter wasn't there.

"Where's the envelope?" I said to myself in light panic. I sorted through the ocean of papers, sure that the letter was lost among the copies of projection notes.

"What's the matter, dear? Your face has completely flushed," Dottie said with a look of concern.

"It's missing. It's gone!" I declared, picking up the whole stack of papers and shaking them, hoping an envelope would fall out.

"What is?" Dottie asked.

"The letter!" I said with more force than I had intended. Dottie flinched ever so slightly at my outburst, not out of fear but out of concern that something was so wrong.

"The one from this morning?" she said, suddenly at attention. "Well, don't worry, dear. I'm sure it's here. We'll find it." She scurried behind my desk to check the drawers as well as the space behind them. Nothing.

"This is unreal," I said, as my anxiety rose.

"Henry, you haven't left the office once today," Dottie reminded me, placing a hand on my cheek. "It's here, and we'll find it." I nodded my head and took a few deep breaths. I picked up the stack of papers again and tried my best to sort through them without getting flustered.

Dottie and I must have searched for another half hour before finally giving up. I had gone through the mountain of papers more than a hundred times. It was no use. The letter was lost. I was filled with more despair than I had felt in a long time. I knew the letter was likely Opal's final goodbye, which was something I was not looking forward to reading. But it was still mine to read, my closure to seize.

"I'm sorry, dear," Dottie said, shaking her head and looking at the sorted papers. "I'm afraid it may be lost."

"It's alright," I lied. "I have a feeling I know what it was about." Dottie gave me a sad look. I gathered the papers to form one overwhelming stack and tossed the lot of them into the bottom drawer of my desk.

"Let's just go," I said, feeling completely defeated. Dottie patted my back in sympathy as we walked out together.

"Dancing sounds nice right about now," I said, trying to lighten the mood. Dottie giggled as she buttoned her coat. She knew I was a terrible dancer. We headed towards the doors and exited to our freedom.

As the months passed, I had thankfully forgotten all about Opal's letter. The workload over the summer months only proved to become even busier. Jeffrey continued to give me a heavier workload than the rest. I assumed he was jealous of how much of Dottie's time I preoccupied, but I didn't care. I didn't even really notice, to be honest. I had assumed that my love life was, for the most part, over. And Dottie was, well, Dottie. Only Opal could fill such a lovesick void, and I knew that I couldn't have her.

I didn't think much of Opal during the summer, not because I didn't want to. It was just too painful of a place to drag myself back to. With her forgotten letter lost in the depths of God knows where, I had no reason to busy myself with her memories. It wasn't until that fateful day, December 17th, that I had to think about what I was doing with my life and what I wanted to be doing. It wasn't until that day that I found my way back to Opal.

The holiday season was one of our slower times, as many businesses weren't looking to pay for more than they had to. It was a Monday when Jeffrey called me into his office with a less than cheerful expression. "Henry." He spoke sternly. "I want to thank you for meeting with me today."

"Of course, Sir." Jeffrey stared at me blankly for a few seconds as I took a seat across from him. I couldn't tell if he was building up to say something or just taking a dramatic pause. "What's this about, Sir?"

He sat up straight in his chair and fixed his tie. "Mr. Viefhaus, on behalf of Edmunds and Company, I would like to extend my sincerest apologies for what I'm about to do… As of now, we will no longer be needing your services." I sat there silently for a few moments, not fully understanding what he had just said.

"Excuse me, Sir?" I could feel my leg shaking as the anger inside began to build.

“Due to the slow season, there isn’t any room in our budget for an extra desk clerk. It’s nothing personal, but you are the newest hire here. We thought it only appropriate that you be the first to go.”

“Sir, Christmas is only a week away. I was supposed to go back home to visit my family. You can’t possibly see fit to do this now.”

He shook his head with false remorse. “Unfortunately, the orders came straight from the big men up top. I’m sorry, but my hands were tied on this one.” He stood up and reached his hand out to mine. “I’d like to thank you for all your hard work. We’ll need you to clear out your desk. On behalf of Edmunds and Company, I extend my hand to you.” I stared at his pathetic gesture of respect and stood abruptly to my feet, making sure he knew I wouldn’t shake his hand. I wanted to shout. I wanted to do what I had been dreaming of doing to Jeffrey since he first hired me, deck him one good time. I fixed my jacket and stormed out of his office.

I was fuming as I returned to my desk. Had he no decency? To lay off a man right before Christmas? It was simply despicable. I had saved up almost all the money I needed for a visit back home to see my folks. I needed just two more paychecks, and I could afford to stay through the new year.

I began shoving papers into my briefcase haphazardly as I couldn’t have cared less if they wrinkled. I could feel all the eyes in the office on me. It was humiliating.

Just as I was finishing, Dottie trotted over to my desk, concern stricken across her brow. “Psst! Henry, what are you doing? What’s going on?” I shook my head at her and continued to pack my things. I searched through the top two drawers only to find a few old notepads and a couple of ink pens that I’d brought from home.

“Not now, Dottie.” I glanced up at her with a stern expression. “I’ve just been fired.” Her expression was speechless. She sighed as she pulled out a cigarette and lit the tail end. She stared at me blankly, trying to make sense of it all. I chuckled to myself. The shock of it wasn’t that surprising if I thought about it. Jeffrey never really liked me, and I guess I knew somewhere deep down that this was not a forever job. But what was I to do now?

Dottie tried her best to whisper despite her current state of shock. "Fired! On what grounds? Oh, that Jeffrey gets me so cross."

"Budget cuts, apparently," I said, focusing on filling my briefcase. Dottie shook her head as she glared back at Jeffrey's office. He watched us through the glass, as he always paid more attention when Dottie was at my desk.

"No. That's not an option. The quarter is almost over, and by January, the company budget will be back at its full capacity. Now you march in there and get your job back!" She stamped her foot and gave me a stern look. I shook my head at her and smiled as I opened the bottom drawer to my desk and sifted through more papers.

"Even if I could, I wouldn't give Jeffrey the satisfaction of begging for my job. Anyhow, I don't want it back." Dottie watched me as I cleared out all the old papers from the bottom drawer. I pulled out a stack and tapped them against the desk to organize them. They were almost completely aligned when an envelope fell out of the stack and onto the desk. Confused, I set aside the bundle of papers on the desk and picked up the envelope to read the name, Opal Pleasant.

My heart froze, just like it did the first time I read her name. How was this possible? I was sure I'd never see that letter again.

"What is that, something for Jeffrey?" Dottie said, reaching out her hand for the letter. I quickly tucked it away in my jacket pocket. She sighed unassumingly and grazed her hand over all the extra papers on my desk. "Hank, what am I gonna do without you? Who's gonna accompany me to work now?"

I sighed back, emerging from my desk with an urgency that could've told anyone I had a secret. I didn't even care about Jeffrey anymore. Seeing that letter from Opal reminded me that I needed to take control of my own life. It was such a strange thing to realize that I was in charge of my destiny. The thought sent a chill across my shoulders.

"I have to go." I squeezed her arm warmly and slung my jacket over my shoulders and quickly stretched my hands through the sleeves.

"Dottie, you're an incredible friend. Thank you for everything." Her eyes beamed like she knew I wasn't wrong.

"Oh, I suppose you're right, Henry dear." She patted my chest and smoothed out my shoulder pads. "Don't be a stranger now. You be sure and visit me sometime." She pecked my cheek and swayed back to her desk. I grabbed my briefcase and bolted for the door.

I was almost running to the bus stop, eager for a place where I could sit down and finally read Opal's letter. I wasn't going to miss the chance to read her words a second time. I didn't care about whatever was awaiting me. No matter what it said, I was determined to fight. I was going to win her back.

The bus arrived as I was running up. I quickly boarded and paid my fare, stealing a free seat by the window. Immediately, I unpackaged the letter from its casing. I desperately needed to read her words. I tried to catch my breath as I read.

St. Louis MS
1309 Howard St.
March 21, 1928

Dear Henry,

My dear, long-lost sweetheart, I am saying this because I don't think you will ever trust me again. Henry, I have spent months finding out where you are. Now that I have found out, I am writing to you though this letter may not be received. But Henry, I just had to write to you. Please don't ignore this letter, as it deserves to be, because if you do, my heart will be broken. I guess you don't care as I have treated you so dirty. But Henry, I have shed many tears over the way I have treated you. And oh, I did want to ask you to forgive me the night you came to talk to me at Laura's New Year's party. But my pride kept me back.

I have often wondered if it hurt you very bad to have to give up on us. I've wondered if it hurt you half as bad as it did me. Oh, Henry, just what words could ever bring you back to me. Do you ever think of me? Do I ever cross your mind? Do you ever sit and wonder where your darling little sweetheart is and if she will ever come back to you? Or have you put me entirely out of your mind, never to think about me again? Henry, have I killed the love you used to have for me? Do I ever exist in your dreams? If so, won't you write me a few lines and tell me how you are and how you have been since last we saw each other?

If you can't ever love me again, I will understand. But Henry, just know that I'll be loving you always with a love that's true always. Please write to a sad-hearted, little girl who is far away from you but one who has yearned and yearned for your heart. It shall never belong to anyone else but you, though they may claim it. Please, darling one, write to me, won't you please?

I am so lonesome for you. Just one line would put my heart in its place again. For Henry, it is so broken I just can't live like this. I am always yours.

Opal.

Please answer soon, will you?

Chapter Three

Opal

"Oh, Christmas tree, oh, Christmas tree, da-da da-da-da duh-duh duh!" My twin sisters, Nettie and Hettie, were singing and dancing through the halls with garland wrapped around their necks like scarves. Mama had asked us to take down all the Christmas decorations while she made dinner. Nettie and Hettie were not as responsible as I was when it came to proper housekeeping. They danced through the halls pretending to be at some formal ball while I undressed the tree and tried not to laugh at their ridiculous getups. It was because I was the eldest; I had to be more sensible and diligent with my chores. Mama told me it was good practice for me since I was now a decent age to marry and care for a home of my own.

"Alright now, girls. Settle down. You've had your fun." Mama came walking into the living room from the kitchen as she cleaned her hands with her apron. "Go wash up for supper, the both of you." Nettie and Hettie giggled and trailed away down the hall. Mama patted Nettie on the bottom as they left. I smiled at Mama as she crossed over and stepped into the living room.

She had a calming way about her. She reached for a red bulb from the tree, decorated in gold glitter and speckled with little white dots of paint. It was one of the most beautiful ornaments that our family owned. Mama didn't like to waste money on decorations that were only used once a year, so every Christmas, we would buy one decorative bulb to hang on the tree. We'd add it to our collection of handmade ones. The tree was mostly dressed with pinecones that the twins and I would stain with paint leftover from painting the fence around our garden out back. "And how are you getting along in here?"

"Just fine, Mama. The tree is nearly finished, and Thomas will be able to break it up for firewood as soon as I'm through." Mama gave me a concerned side-eye as I said this. I sighed and tried not to pay attention to her silent remarks.

"Ah, and where is Thomas?" She placed another bulb in the decorations box and folded her arms.

"He stepped out to run an errand." I fought hard to escape her eye; I knew what she was going to say. It put my stomach in knots just to think of it. My eyes darted to the floor for solace.

"Opal." Her voice was stern now. She stepped towards me and pulled my chin up so that my eyes met hers. "Have you thought about what I said? It's about time you made a decision. You're not getting any younger, darling." A single tear fell down my cheek, and I pulled away from her in a dramatic fit.

"Oh, Mother, how could you make me do it! How could you possibly think I could marry Thomas?" I crossed my arms and planted myself on the sofa, wiping my endless tears with my apron. She walked over to me with a callous expression and sat beside me. She wrapped her arms around me and held tightly.

"Oh, for Heaven's sake, Opal. Now don't be so dramatic!" She rocked me slowly and rubbed my head as I cried. I sat up straight and looked at her straight in the eyes.

"But, Mama, I don't love Thomas, not the way I love Henry. I'm going to be with Henry."

"Opal, dear. I want to believe you, but it's been almost nine months since you sent Henry that letter, and even longer since you've seen him. I think it's time that you accept that Henry's moved on. He left Missouri to start his new life in

California." Her words stung my very core. I didn't want to believe her, but I feared she was right. How could Henry possibly love me after the terrible way I treated him before he left? I cried harder into Mama's arms. "So, it's settled then, hmm? You'll accept Thomas' proposal?" I squeezed her arm and imagined my life with Thomas 'The Doctor.' I was to be the housewife of a prestigious doctor who would take care of me for the rest of my life. I would bare his children, keep his house and have everything that I've always wanted with my Henry, but with Thomas. I nodded once and let go of Mama's embrace.

"If it will please the family," I groan, as Mama stood to her feet and kissed my forehead.

"It will. Oh, Opal, you are going to be so happy. The rest of your life starts now," Mama beamed. She gave me a tight hug and then steadied her eyes on mine. "Opal, look at me. You will learn to love him. I promise." Just then, we heard the front door open. It was Thomas, back from his errand. I quickly wiped the tears from my face and returned to the tree to finish taking down the decorations. Mama walked back towards the kitchen to finish dinner just as Nettie and Hettie re-appeared from upstairs.

"Opal, your betrothed is here!" Nettie teased as she made kissing noises at me. I rolled my eyes as Thomas walked in to greet me. He was a tall man, not as tall as Henry but tall enough. His eyes looked tired behind his spectacles, and his blonde hair was beginning to thin and recede away from his hairline. He was only 29, but his face had already aged so much. I was going to be the 18-year-old wife of a tired, old doctor.

"Hello, darling. I see you're nearly finished now." He kissed my cheek, and I gave him a curt grin. Nettie and Hettie stretched out beside the fireplace with paper and pencil and began to draw. Thomas sensed our audience and lowered his voice to me. "Opal, dear. Have you thought any more about my proposal?" My stomach tied into knots once again. I steadied my breath. I turned toward the tree and continued to unhook bulbs, hoping he wouldn't see my unenthused expression.

"I have."

"And? Have you come up with an answer for me?" Henry's face raced across my thoughts. I loved Henry. I would always love Henry. Even if I married Thomas and bore his children, my heart would always belong to Henry. But I also knew that Henry went to California to begin his future, not his past. And I was Henry's past. A knock at the door interrupted my thoughts.

"Oh, who could be at the door at this hour? It's almost seven-thirty." I pretended to be annoyed by the interruption, but I couldn't have been more thankful for it. I slipped out of the living room and down the hall toward the front door, glad to escape Thomas for a moment. To my surprise, it was Ray Carter. He was engaged to my dear friend Laura. He was breathing heavily and leaning against the doorframe.

"Ray? What are you doing here? Is it Laura? Is she alright?" He nodded and shooed my remarks.

"Oh, Laura's fine. I'm sorry to bother you this time of night, but I wanted to catch you before your family turned in for the evening."

"Well, what is it?" He removed an envelope from his coat pocket and handed it to me. I could feel Thomas approaching as Ray caught his breath. His presence made my ears warm. I just wished he would leave me alone.

"It's for you." I read the name on the envelope and almost fainted at the sight of what I read.

"Is everything alright, Opal?" Thomas asked as he approached. I quickly tucked the envelope under my apron and grinned at Thomas as he anchored himself next to me.

"Yes, dear. This is just a dear friend from school. He was dropping by to say hello." Thomas checked his watch pretentiously and made a sour face at Ray.

"It's a little late to be making a house call, wouldn't you say so? Uh, I'm sorry. I didn't get your name."

"It's Ray, and again, I apologize for the hour. I was just leaving. I guess I'll see you around, Opal." Ray smiled politely, backing away slowly as he turned to patter down the porch steps. I closed the door and clenched tightly to the letter under my apron. Thomas raised his brow at me expecting an explanation at once.

"He was just passing along a message from my dear friend, Laura." He folded his arms and huffed.

"Why couldn't Laura do so herself?" I shrugged my shoulders defensively.

"It isn't proper for a lady to be out this time of night. Wouldn't you agree?" He wrapped his palms around my shoulders and squeezed tightly.

"Opal, I'm allowed to be a little angry that other men are coming to visit you, especially ones that are visiting after sundown. Now, I expect a real answer from you. Tell me, right now!" His tone was tense, and it made me uneasy. I shoved him away and glared as hard as I could.

"You are not my father that I need to answer to you!" I stormed up the stairs just as Mama appeared in the hall with wide eyes.

"What is the meaning of all this hysteria?" she yelled. I stopped halfway up and took in a deep breath as I looked back at Mama. My eyes were filled with tears once again, but this time out of complete rage. By this time, even the twins had joined us in the hall to see what all the fuss was. Mama saw my expression and pointed a finger at me. "Opal, you stop this behavior right now. I won't tolerate this kind of sass in my house!"

I raced up the stairs and into my room, burying my face in my pillow. I could hear Mama's muffled voice from below. "I apologize, Thomas. I know you planned to stay for supper, but perhaps it's best if you leave."

"I'm afraid you're right, Mrs. Pleasant. I apologize for all the commotion." Thomas said something else to Mama under his breath that I couldn't quite make out. After some quiet mumbling between the two, I could hear Thomas' footsteps fading towards the door and then an abrupt slam that shook the whole house.

I didn't care that he left. I huffed deeply as I tried to stay calm. I had never seen Thomas with such a temper. I squeezed the letter under my apron again. It had crumpled a little in my hand. I pulled it out to read the name once again. Henry Viefhaus. There it was in plain black ink, my sign in the sky.

Chapter Four

Opal

San Pedro, CA
December 28, 1928

My Dearest Opal,

I am sorry. I just now received your letter, but I would love to hear from you as soon as possible. I hope you can forgive me for all the heartache I put you through back home. I beg you to forgive me, Opal. And if you can find it in your heart to forgive me, may you also find the time to write me a few lines as well? I've always loved you, and as God is my witness, I swear to you that one day we will be together. I am going to marry you, Opal Pleasant.

Yours always,

Henry

The smell of sweet-savory sausage and eggs filled the air. My eyes shifted gently under their lids as the aroma charmed me to wake. The smell brought me back to when I was a little girl. How much easier things were then. The thought of mama hoisting me up on a stool to help her beat eggs for breakfast floated through my mind as the memories soothed me. I smiled as I turned over in my bed. I must have fallen asleep without realizing because I could feel my pleated skirt beneath my stomach, bunching up and creating a knot just above my navel. If Mama knew, she'd yell at me something fierce. She hated it when we slept in our dresses. I smiled to myself as I let the sunshine wash over me from the window.

"That dress is probably ruined, Opal. I'll probably have to steam it to get the wrinkles out." My eyes shot open at the sound of Mama's voice from inside my room. I had no idea she was even upstairs. It was almost as if she could hear my thoughts exactly. I looked over to find her sitting in the chair across from my bed. Her voice sounded normal, but her expression told me she was concerned about something. I sat up in my bed and swung my legs over, so they dangled over the edge. I could feel the laces from my brown boots still hugging my calves. I looked down at them and then back up at Mama playfully. She gave me a look like she was not amused. She sat in the chair next to my bedroom door with her hands neatly clasped in her lap, almost as if she was attempting to hide her fuller frame from me. Her dark brown hair was pulled back into a loose bun behind her head. She was already dressed for the day, but she hadn't a spot of makeup on. The deep lines at the corners of her eyes gave away her age.

"I-I'm sorry, Mama. I can steam it myself if you like," I said uneasy. She shook her head at me and forced a smile. I couldn't tell if she was sad or cross with me.

"You missed supper last night." She squinted her eyes at me, trying to understand my hidden thoughts. "I sent the girls up to get you, but they said you had fallen asleep with your day clothes on. You must be famished."

I nodded and rose from the springs of my bed. "Yes, ma'am." I scratched my head and stretched my arms high up above my head. “I suppose I was more exhausted than I assumed.”

“Oh, for heaven’s sake, Opal, don’t just stand there stretching and yawning like some poor, classless beggar.” Her face had scrunched to an unflattering point, and she pursed her lips at me and scoffed. “Are you a lady, or aren’t you?” I nodded my head and quickly stood up straight. Mama rose to her feet and met me in the center of my bedroom, glaring me right in the eye. “Now you listen to me, Opal Pleasant. That nonsense from last night, I won’t have any part of it. Understood?” Now I knew why she had been so difficult to read. She was referring to the whole affair with Thomas from the night before. The thought of Thomas put my stomach in knots, not the good kind where your heart accompanies it with faint flutters. Thomas made me just plain sick. He was all show in front of Mama, but a different man when it was just us two. Mama gave me a stern look one last time before turning and heading for the door. “Get cleaned up, child. Breakfast is just about ready.”

I nodded and snuck in a yawn behind her back. She turned just as I was finishing up a grand stretch. I jolted back into the appropriate upright position and gave her an embarrassed grin. She kept herself from grinning back at me and quickly shut the door behind herself. I rolled my eyes when she left and fell back flat on my bedspread. My bangs fell to my face and covered my eyes. I let out a puff of air, and they flew backward, slowly cascading down to form a perfect frame around my face. I laid still for a moment, taking in the dramatic events of the night before. Was I dreaming? Had Henry really written me that letter? I quickly sat up and dug through my tousled blankets in search of the letter. I found it peeking from beneath my pillow. Drawing the smooth paper from its hiding place, I began to read, drinking in Henry’s words again. It was real. Henry had written to me. Henry was still thinking of me. The thought of him made me involuntarily blush.

“Opal Pleasant, I don’t want to have to call your name again!” Mama yelled from downstairs. I startled from my daze and quickly pulled the pins from my hair to readjust them into place.

"Yes, Mama, I'll be right there!" I sat down at the little desk in the corner of my room with the vanity mirror attached. The vanity was a present from my papa when I turned 15. He gave it to me just before he passed. Mama told him it was too adult for a 15-year-old girl to have a vanity. She argued it would only make me worry about my looks before I needed to. But Papa never listened; he was always looking for some way to spoil me.

I often thought of my papa. I missed him more than anything. His death was sudden and unexpected, which made it even more painful. One moment he was fine, as healthy as ever. Then, seemingly out of nowhere, he got sick. Doctor Sherman said he had a bad case of pneumonia. Papa was placed on bed rest indefinitely as Doctor Sherman worked hard to make my papa well again. He was making house calls three to four times a week. But Doctor Sherman's efforts were to no avail. Within weeks we lost him. Mama was there to pick up the pieces, never once letting on how devastated she was.

I willed the painful memory away as I stared at myself in the oval mirror across from me. I pinned back a stray curl that was hanging over my eye. I suddenly felt beautiful. I was well aware of my appearance. I had often heard people whisper about me when they thought I paid no attention. Once, I heard Bailey Adams, a girl two years younger than I am, whisper to another girl one Sunday during church that Thomas was so lucky to have gotten a girl like me to talk to him. Mama quickly turned around and scolded them for speaking out of turn, and during the Reverend's sermon no less. I smiled to myself, trying to keep my flattery hidden. After the service, Mama told me that it's not polite nor will it do me any good to think so highly of myself.

Looking at my slender face and button nose in the mirror now, I couldn't help but to think highly of myself. Even the thought of Henry's hands writing a letter to me, even after everything I did to push him away, sent a chill across my shoulders. I smoothed down my eyebrows and smiled sweetly at myself. A rush of embarrassment flooded over me, and I had to look away. I floated over to my bed and picked up the letter one more time to read over his last words. 'Yours Always, Henry.' He was mine, and by some miracle of fate, I was still his.

I smoothed the bedspread and tucked the letter beneath my pillow again for safekeeping. "Opal Pleasant! Is this disobedience going to become a habit?" My eyes widened, and I trotted towards Mama's angry voice, which was growing more impatient from downstairs.

"No, ma'am. Be right there!"

Breakfast was short. We only had three eggs to feed the four of us, and the two sausages had to be cut in half to make sure we all had at least one piece. Nettie and Hettie ate their breakfast in unison, bringing their forks to their mouths in a synchronized motion and giggling each time they took a bite. "Just because you're twins doesn't mean you have to do the same things." Nettie scoffed at me, and Hettie glared from behind her glass of milk.

"Says who? We like doing the same things." I rolled my eyes at them as I stood to wash my dishes. I could feel Mama eyeing me from the table, looking for a chance to make a dig at me.

"Thomas will be by today," she said pointedly, waiting to hear my response. I purposefully kept myself from reacting to her comment.

"Oh? That should be nice." Mama took a sip of her tea and clinked the glass back together with its matching saucer.

"...along with the Reverend Stone. They should be by around four this evening to discuss the arrangements." At this, I turned to her both confused and outraged all at once.

"Arrangements? Is there something to make arrangements for?" I already knew what she was referring to, but I wanted to hear her say the words with her own lips. I wanted to hear Mama say that she was going to force me into a marriage that any blind person could've seen was all wrong.

"Well, for the wedding, of course. Thomas thought it might be a good idea to bring Reverend Stone along for some pre-marital counseling." She took another sip from her teacup, but I knew she wasn't thirsty. She was trying to make clear her dominance over me. The twins looked at Mama and then back to me, wondering what I might say to arrangements for a marriage I hadn't even declared a proper yes to. I held my tongue, even though at that moment, I could have well blown up right there in the kitchen. And no one could have questioned it. I walked over to the table and stacked the twins' plates together. Then I walked confidently back to the sink to wash them.

"Well, of course." I gritted the words through my teeth as I scrubbed the dishes harder than they needed for breakfast as light as eggs and a small piece of sausage. "That's a fine idea." I turned the plates face down on a towel to dry and paced out of the kitchen before I lost all composure. "I'd better wash up. I wouldn't dream of Thomas seeing me in the same dress as last night."

"Don't dawdle, girl. I need you to run to town to pick up a few things for me before they arrive."

"Yes, Mama," I called back from the hall as tears burned my cheeks in a race to get to my chin. They stained my lip, and I wiped them bitterly with the back of my hand. I stomped up the stairs without even the slightest worry that Mama would come after me, as I was undoubtedly sure that she knew she had gotten to me. I plopped down at my vanity desk and stared at myself hard, scrunching my brows together and forming a wrinkle in my forehead. The beauty I saw before had vanished. I felt like a poor girl with no means for the nicer things in life. I made a pillow with my arms across the desk and lay my head down between them, trying to muffle my cries.

"Opal?" Hettie's voice was soft and sweet, but I was in no mood to entertain the twins. I sat up straight and looked at her through the mirror of the vanity as she peeked her head in the doorway. The only part of her showing was her head. Her light brown hair was curled to perfection. All Mama's doing, I assumed, on account of the Reverend coming to visit. I wiped a tear from my lip and sniffled loudly.

"What is it, Hettie?" Nettie popped her head in underneath Hettie's. Her hair curled in exactly the same way. Hettie rested her head on Nettie's, and they both stared back at me with eyes wide.

"Are you upset because you don't want to marry Thomas?" Hettie pressed. I shook my head at them and mopped up another tear with my sleeve.

"It's complicated, girls. I'm a woman now. It's not about want; it's about need." Nettie cocked her head slightly in confusion.

"So, you need to marry Thomas?" Nettie continued. I sighed without meaning to and nodded at them. I stood up from the desk and walked over to my door to shoo them away. "Why would you need to marry him?"

"It's because he's a doctor, Nettie. Don't be stupid," said Hettie. Nettie rolled her eyes and stood up straight in the doorway, forcing Hettie to move her chin from atop her head. I wagged a finger at Hettie as I reached for the door.

"Don't talk to your sister that way, Hettie. Now you girls go away. I'm in no mood for this now." I closed the door. I could hear their small boots clicking down the hallway against the wooden floors as they skipped to their bedroom.

I sighed, staring back at my room so empty of life. My only possessions were a small, one-person bed with a worn wooden frame pushed up beside the window, a tall dresser that stood beside it with woodwork that matched the design of the bed frame and the vanity that Papa got me in the corner of the room. The vanity was by far the most beautiful part of the entire bedroom. It had been properly sanded and varnished, not like the bed frame and dresser, which gave me splinters if I rubbed them against the grain. Even the matching stool had been varnished and detailed with unique carvings of roses on the legs. Finally, there was the random and out of place chair sitting by the door that was meant to go in the dining room downstairs at the formal dining table. The dining room was smaller than Papa realized when he bought the table, so they put the extra chair in my room.

I decided that I would lift my spirits before the day was done. Not Mama, nor Thomas or even the Reverend Stone himself, for that matter, were going to keep me in a sour mood.

I was walking my way into town down the main road by the time Mama had finished cleaning up the rest of the dishes from breakfast. I had my favorite dress on, the sky-blue one with the white buttons that traced up my back, paired with my nicest brown walking pumps. They had a neatly tied leather bow at the top just where my ankle showed. I smiled at my feet as they involuntarily danced along the sidewalk. They were the shoes I bought the day I met Henry, Mr. Penny's Shoes, September 1927. He came in to get a repair done on his work boots. Mama and I had been looking for a new pair of pumps for the upcoming formal held to honor all the soldiers who had fought in the Great War and to celebrate all the young soldiers enlisting. Mama thought it would be a great place to find a husband or *secure my future,* as she called it. Henry was already inside when we came in, fidgeting with the uprooting sole of one of his shoes and trying to haggle with Mr. Penny for a lower price. Mama and I walked in and started searching right away for the perfect shoe. We walked past Henry and Mr. Penny to a section in the back of the store. Displayed on a table were my shoes and an identical pair in black. Mama wasted no time calling over Mr. Penny to ask for help with sizing. It was then that Henry looked up. He noticed me almost as instantly as I did him. Our eyes fixated on one another as Mr. Penny and Mama gabbed about how many pairs he had in stock. He walked over slowly to me without any time to lose. I remember blushing at his forwardness.

"Hello." He flashed a confident smile at me, revealing the most beautiful set of teeth I had ever seen. He took a moment to examine me. I could feel his eyes dancing over my hair, my cheeks, my nose, and then back to my eyes. He was taking it all in, and so was I. "Wow, you are beautiful, aren't you?" I gave him a bashful smile. I didn't say anything back. I couldn't. I had never been approached this way before. My words forsook me, and all I was left with was a dainty smile. I quickly gave him a polite nod and glided past him to find Mama. By this point, she had already prompted Mr. Penny to bring her three different styles of shoes for me to try. Henry didn't follow. I imagine he must have embarrassed himself when I didn't reply to his compliment. But I could feel his eyes on me as I tried on the first pair of shoes.

Mr. Penny returned to Henry's aid and told him he'd have his shoe repaired by the end of the week. Henry thanked him and pocketed his receipt. Our eyes connected as he trailed to the doors. I didn't know if he was delighted or disappointed, but he stared a long while before finally taking his exit out the doors. I could feel a tingling in my cheeks as they flushed to red. I watched his shadow disappear outside. "Hurry up, Opal! We haven't got all day!" Mama hadn't even noticed where my gaze had wandered. "That daydreaming mind of yours is going to be your downfall if you don't break that silly habit now." I fixed my eyes back down to the brown pumps and fastened them tightly, so as not to hear any more of Mama's complaints. I stood up to try them out, taking a few steps to make sure they were comfortable. The bells that hung on Mr. Penny's front door jingled at the inward push of the entrance door. I did a spin for Mama. She smiled as I playfully did a little bit of the Charleston step. I didn't pay any attention to the new customer that had entered until I spun around only to see Henry standing behind me with a silly grin stuck on his jawline. I immediately stopped and turned back towards Mama. Gently, he reached out for my arm before I could get to safety and turned me back around to face him.

"You're quite the dancer. I'm sure you get compliments all the time for your dancing." I nodded politely and smiled with my eyes. I could hear Mama clearing her throat and chuckling, delighted to see that I had already gotten the attention of a handsome fellow. I ignored her ticklish giggles and tried to focus on not fainting from my humiliation.

"I don't get to go dancing very often," I said shyly, being sure not to make contact with his inquisitive eyes.

"Ah, well, that's a shame, seeing as how you're so good at it." I let out a small giggle and attempted to regain some of my abandoned confidence. "Perhaps I could take you some time. We could even go tonight if you like!" He crossed his arms, considering his idea. His eyes beamed with excitement. I looked back at Mama, who, at this point, was pretending to busy herself with putting the shoes back in their rightful boxes. She looked up at me and smiled. I turned back towards Henry.

"Well, I was supposed to attend the *Soldier's Appreciation Formal Dinner* this evening." His eyes dropped for a slight moment and then quickly lit back up. There was a kindness to him that I couldn't overlook. He was so endearing, even at our first meet. "Perhaps, I'll see you there?" I encouraged, wondering if he might come and find me. He nodded and let out an accomplished sigh.

"Perhaps, you will. I think I'd be pretty stupid not to take another chance to see a girl as lovely as you, now wouldn't I?" I giggled at him and let my eyes wander over his face. I could tell he was older than I was, but not by much. His head was full of beautiful brown hair that had been combed almost perfectly. He stood about a foot taller than me and wore a cleanly pressed, sack suit, brown with gold buttons.

"I suppose you would be Mister, uh, what was it?" He extended his hand out to mine and held it ever so gently.

"Viefhaus. Henry Viefhaus. Pleasure. And your name is?" I gave him my eyes with as much poise as I could muster.

"Opal." I withdrew my hand from his and locked my arms behind my back. "Opal Pleasant."

He chuckled. "Beautiful name for a beautiful lady." He disappeared almost as quickly as he had entered. I turned back to Mama. Excited and bashful were permanently written in my eyes. Mama just laughed and turned back to Mr. Penny, who had been watching the interaction from behind his register at the desk.

"We'll take the ones she's wearing, Mr. Penny. I'm beginning to think there's a bit of luck sewn into the soles." Mr. Penny and Mama shared a laugh as he rung up the shoes.

I smiled to myself as I reminisced that day, stepping down from the sidewalk to cross the narrow road into town. The morning air was brisk, and a slight breeze was kicking up the leaves that had fallen and hardened into orange flakes on the ground. When I reached town, the streets were already busied with automobiles and people walking the freshly paved sidewalks of downtown. I pulled the list of items I was supposed to get for Mama from my pocket. They were all ingredients for the meal she was planning to prepare for Thomas and the Reverend. A whole chicken and potatoes were scribbled in as a last-minute addition at the bottom of the list. I rolled my eyes. Mama must have been planning a feast for the two of them, something to impress them with her hospitality and knowledge of spices.

I walked by the post office, just a few stores away from the market. I almost hadn't noticed it until I spotted a young couple inside from the window. They were laughing with the mail attendant as the gentleman handed him an envelope. I thought about Henry. I craved that feeling of perpetual happiness. I was drawn inside by their laughter. I walked along the back wall looking at all of the displayed office items. They had stamps, envelopes, rubber bands, paper clips and stationery - decorative and plain white. My hand smoothed over one of the decorative papers; it had roses in both corners at the top and perfect lines that paralleled one another below. The couple thanked the attendant and drifted out the doors. I reached in my pocket for Henry's letter. I wouldn't have dared to leave it behind with those meddling twins. I ran my fingers over the smooth paper and withdrew it from my jacket to look at it one more time.

"Trying to pick the right stationery for a special someone?" Startled, I turned my gaze up to the mailing attendant. He was a short, little man, but his uniform fit him nicely. He seemed like such a strange older fellow with hair so fine. It seemed like his platinum yellow hair was beginning to thin out and bald; after a closer look, I wondered if maybe it was.

"Oh, no. Just admiring your beautiful selection." I smiled politely and started for the exit.

"You sure, Miss? I couldn't believe a sweet young thing like yourself doesn't have a romance brewing this time o' year. You know Valentine's is just around the corner." I nodded sweetly at the kind old gentleman and turned my gaze back towards the rose stationery. I thought about how furious Mama would be with me if I returned with less change than she'd expected. I imagined what Thomas might do if he found out I was writing Henry. The thought of Thomas made me angry; I wanted to spite him with anything I could.

"Well, maybe just one letter. I do love this one with the roses."

"Excellent choice, Miss. Let me get you something to write with. You just stay put." The little man bounced away and disappeared behind the counter. I sighed with hopefulness. Maybe Henry wouldn't take so long to write back this time. Perhaps reading my words would move him so deeply that he'd rush back to St. Louis to marry me and free me from my nightmare with Thomas. Maybe.

Chapter Five

Henry

St. Louis, MO
January 10, 1929

Henry, oh, how I've missed you so. My heart did a leap when your sweet letter was delivered to me. I knew somehow that we would find our way back to each other. I knew that God would one day bring you back to me, my darling mine. My heart is glad to read your words, my love, and to spend my life with you is all I want. But I'm afraid Mama's plans to have me marry Thomas may prove to ruin our hopes to be together. Do you remember him, dear, Thomas Laverne and his family of doctors? They do have a nice enough family, but they are no fit for me. I am going to fight, Henry. I am going to wait as long as I can for you, my love. Please don't leave me alone for very long, or I fear Mama will have no choice but to give Thomas my hand. The garden doesn't produce many vegetables these days. There hasn't been a real way for Mama to make money. Mama thinks my marrying Thomas is the only way to bring income back into the house. My humble little wages from the printing shop are not nearly enough. I hate having to discuss money, but I fear Mama already has her heart set on Thomas. Oh, please, Henry dear, won't you come back to me? Save your darling girl from this terrible dream. I love you, Henry. And I will wait for you. Just don't be long, my dear.

Yours truly,

Opal Pleasant

My eyes burned as I read over Opal's words. I tried to remember this Thomas fellow whom she had referred to in her letter. I snapped my fingers as it came to me. "Doctor Laverne! Oh, that witty bastard!"

"Everything alright, Henry?" I turned to Herman, my now concerned older brother. He stood a few feet away from me on the sidewalk outside of his apartment building, furniture surrounding us. I had to move out of the room I was renting from an elderly man on account of my getting fired. Herman had so kindly offered up the spare bedroom of his apartment while I looked for work. He had already been in California for two years. He was making decent wages as a longshoreman on the San Pedro docks. A bead of sweat was hanging over his brow as he focused his eyes on me, ready to hear me assure him that I was fine. I nodded at him as I watched his shoulders ease.

"Fine. Just got a letter from Opal." I waved the paper at him and then stuffed it into my pocket. "It would appear that she may be dangerously close to a betrothal." Herman widened his eyes at the sound of this and scoffed.

"She's getting engaged?"

"Not if I can prevent it." I walked over to him and retrieved the now crumpled letter from my pocket.

"Who's the suitor?"

I wiped my forehead with the back of my hand and shielded my eyes from the sun. "He's an older fellow, Thomas Laverne. Do you remember the Laverne Family?" Herman shook his head in disbelief.

“That old geezer? Opal would never willingly take a proposal from him!” I nodded my head in agreement, feeling almost completely defeated.

“That’s just the thing. It seems that her mother is arranging it all. He’s a doctor, so he’s well off.” I let out a sigh, not even bothering to hide my sorrow from Herman. “I’ve got to find work, and very soon, I’m afraid.” Herman patted my back sympathetic to the cause. I scratched my head and looked around at the furniture sitting on the sidewalk. It wasn’t much, just two side tables and a mattress. Hidden inside a drawer of one of the side tables was the small box my father had sent me a few months ago. I had never even opened it. Herman didn’t know about it. The only person aware that I had received the package was Dottie, and by now, I’m sure she had forgotten.

Herman bent down and used his knees to lift one of the dressers off the ground. “C’mon, bud. Aren’t you gonna help your poor, old brother with the rest of this?” I chuckled and nodded at him. He was straining as I reached down and picked up the other small table. I followed Herman up the stairs running along the side of the building and onto the second floor as we headed inside his place. Luckily his apartment was the first one on the corner, so we didn’t have to travel too far. We set the side tables down in the spare bedroom and took a minute to catch our breath. Herman came out of his struggle for air quicker than I did.

“You know what you need?” He pointed a finger at me like he was about to settle all my problems at once. “Whiskey!” I folded my arms and looked at him with questioning eyes.

“Whiskey? What do you mean whiskey?” I knew what he meant, but with the prohibition going on, I knew there were scarce ways to get it, most of them illegal. He wagged his finger at me and rubbed his hands together like he was cooking up trouble for the two of us.

“Ah, ah, ah. There’s a speakeasy not too far from here. That’s what you need!” He did a quick skip and adjusted his waistband. I weighed the option in my mind, but I knew that illegal alcohol could be dangerous. The last thing I needed was trouble. Herman continued to excite himself over the idea of it all. “C’mon little Brother. It’ll be an adventure! We’ll have some drinks. We'll get a little dinner, and we'll charm the ladies." He raised his eyebrows up and down when he said this, like he was the king of romance. He grabbed my hand. He began leading me around the room in a simple two-step, pretending that I was an eligible bachelorette. He hummed a light jazz tune and made saxophone noises as he attempted to spin me. I rolled my eyes and laughed at his silly amusements. Herman always was the most humorous of all our siblings. He always knew how to put a smile on a gloomy face.

I broke away from his foolish dance and put my hands up in surrender. "Alright, alright. I give in. Where is this speakeasy?" Herman clapped his hands together in accomplishment.

"Yes! That's why you're my favorite brother!" He kissed my forehead and danced out of the room, humming that same tune as he left. "We leave at sunset!" I chuckled to myself as I looked around my new bedroom. It was a quaint space, but I knew it would work. I headed back outside for the mattress, hoping no one had picked it up, mistaking it for garbage. Although, it wouldn't have been the worst thing to happen if someone had. It was a terrible mattress, stained and tearing at the seams. I struggled to drag it up the stairs by myself. I caught myself having visions of Opal as I hoisted the mattress through the living room and into my room. One day Opal and I would do this same thing when we moved into our first home together, one day soon if I have anything to do with it.

Herman and I finished unpacking my things rather quickly, finishing by four o'clock. At five o'clock, we were already having our shoes polished for the night. I wore my best tan suit and a freshly polished pair of brown dress shoes. I don't know why I was so dressed up; it wasn't like I intended to meet a lady. Nevertheless, I put on my Sunday best. Herman wore an all-black suit with black shoes, simple, but always classic.

"So, where is this speakeasy exactly?" The bus bounced along over the night's gravel roads. Herman widened his eyes at me.

"Keep it down. Will ya? Gee, you want the whole town to know what we're up to?" I nodded my head at him in agreement and waited for him to tell me. Herman leaned in close enough so that his whispers couldn't be heard. "There's a joint in downtown Venice that has an underground bar. You can only get to it through the back door where the shipments come in, and you have to know the password."

"Well, how do you suppose we get that?" Herman pulled out a small napkin from his pocket; it had the word *persuasion* scribbled on it in girlish handwriting. He grinned at me as I read it. "Persuasion? That's the secret word?"

"Sure is, brother. I was waiting until the right time to go. A woman who works at the local diner by my apartment told me she sings there some nights. She told me I should come by and see her some time." Herman winked at me and chuckled as he carefully folded the napkin and stuffed it back in his jacket pocket. "Her name's Millie." I nodded at him, as I quickly understood that this was a chance to impress a girl. After twenty more minutes of bouncing along on busy roads through Venice, we were finally dropped off on Windward Avenue. It seemed that everyone was out that night, probably all looking to have a drink and forget their sorrows for one night. "Alright, it's just a few blocks away." Herman straightened himself in his suit jacket and pulled out a cigar from his inner pocket.

After about ten minutes of following my brother's lead, we finally approached the front of a dark grocery market. There were stores and restaurants surrounding it on both sides, all with their lights turned out for the night. It was a wonder that there were so many couples out with all of the buildings that had been abandoned for the evening. Women skipped by us, linking arms with dear friends while young men offered their coats to any girl who would pay them attention. "Where are all these people going?" I wondered to myself. *Menotti's Grocery* had been painted above the entrance of a small market. Herman pointed to the store and smiled. "Here we are. I knew it couldn't be far."

I looked at the grocery store and then back at Herman. "Herman, this is a grocery market. Am I supposed to believe there's a full-functioning bar inside?"

Herman chuckled as he took a quick drag from his now stubby cigar and puffed out a cloud. "Pardon, Henry, but wouldn't ya say that's the idea?" I chuckled as well at his comment while following him around to the back of the grocery store despite my reservations about every light in the store being out. We came to a door in the back, side alley that was poorly lit by an overhead lamp. Herman knocked three times, taking steady pauses between each one. "Millie says the knock is very important." I nodded as we waited.

After a few more seconds of heightened anticipation, a large gentleman, whose shoulders were as broad as Herman's and mine put together, cracked open the door wide enough so that we could see only his body in the doorway. A cigar hung from his teeth and rested on his bottom lip. "I will ask you this once and only once. Password?" His voice was shockingly deep and hoarse, much deeper than I had expected, even from a man his size.

Herman took a slow drag from his cigar once more before answering, probably to calm his nerves. "Persuasion," he managed to keep himself upright as he spoke. The large gentleman nodded as he opened the door all the way to allow us passage. He eyed us as we stepped inside and led us through the back of the tiny grocery store.

The large man cracked his knuckles as we followed closely. "Alright, gentlemen, don't waste your evening being foolish. If you get in any trouble, you'll have to answer to Mouse."

"Forgive me, but who's Mouse?" Herman tightened his tie as he asked this, most likely thinking the same thing I was. *What are we doing here?*

The large man barely turned his head to answer him, "I'm Mouse. Keep your manners intact, and there shouldn't be any problems. Ya got it?" We both nodded as we turned a corner. We were soon in a small restocking room behind the shelves of the last aisle. Two other large men awaited us, both of them more substantial and taller than Mouse. I wondered how that was even possible. It was no wonder how Mouse had gotten his name because he was the smallest. Mouse pointed to a plain rug on the floor and gave them the thumbs up. "Got two fresh ones for ya. I gotta get back. Just let 'em through. No need for a pat-down." With those last words, Mouse disappeared back through the door we came, leaving Herman and me with the two giants who had yet to introduce themselves.

The tallest man quickly pulled back the plain rug on the floor to reveal a large basement door carved out in the floorboards. Bent on one knee, he cracked open the wooden door and stuffed his head into the darkness of the basement. After a few seconds, a light clicked on, revealing a staircase below. The large man stood and motioned for Herman and me to go in. I hesitated for a moment, but Herman went right on in, not even missing a beat. I went quickly after him to avoid being left alone with the giants. Once we were both inside, we heard the slam of the basement door above us, followed by the sliding of the rug. We followed the narrow hallway to its end, where we could more clearly hear the sounds of light jazz music playing and glasses clinking together. After a few more steps, we could hear the abrupt laughter from within.

Once we were at the end of the hall, we made our way through the opened doorway at the end and planted our eyes on a perfect, fully functioning bar. It was incredible. Before us was a platform stage with a brunette woman singing, a live band, a stocked bar, with booth tables lining the entire perimeter of the basement. The place was filled with men and eligible women all laughing and having the time of their lives.

"Looks like we've stumbled into heaven, my brother!" I smiled as Herman patted my shoulder and then removed his jacket.

"Welcome to *The Del Monte*, gentlemen. May I have your coats?" A petite redheaded woman greeted us where we stood. I quickly removed my coat and handed it over. She escorted us to a booth in the corner and hurried off.

"Look at this place? This is better than any of the ones back home!" Herman was ecstatic. He could barely keep his hands from fidgeting.

I pulled out my pipe and took a match to its bowl. "Mmhmm, I haven't seen a spot like this since Pa took us with him to New York. Say, uh, where's your friend? Weren't you planning on seeing a girl tonight?"

Herman smiled to himself and then pointed proudly to the stage. "The one singin' her heart out. That's Millie." I looked back over to the stage where she was. She wore an all-black cocktail dress and had a jeweled band wrapped around the crown of her head.

I shrugged slightly as I looked at her. She was a pretty one, but all she did was remind me of Opal. It was the first time she had crossed my mind that night. The young singer's thick brown hair only brought me back to the equally beautiful hair that Opal so diligently took care of. She always curled and pinned it just right, making sure that each strand was laid perfectly against the next. Millie finished her song just as she and Herman made eye contact. Herman stood from the table and smoothed his vest. "Don't wait around for me, Hank. I'm gonna be a little preoccupied tonight." With that, he left. I watched Herman and Millie for a few moments. They were quite playful with one another. She reached for his hat and nearly fell into his arms trying to tease him. I was happy for my brother. I really was, but I could also feel a slight envy brewing within.

Looking around the bar, I realized I was surrounded by happy single women all over. Glancing over at the entrance door, I imagined Opal walking through and spotting me. I would run to her side, and we'd dance until our feet hurt. As I was envisioning Opal's shining face in the doorway, to my surprise, another familiar face appeared. Dottie was standing there wearing a shimmery red cocktail dress and holding a matching cigarette holder. No purse, of course, she didn't like dragging them around when she went out on the town, or so she told me. Dottie would always tell me, "It's no use carrying false beauty in a bag, either you got it, or you don't." To my surprise, she was accompanied by Jeffrey, my old boss and Dottie's less-than-secret admirer. He could barely let go of her arm long enough for her to remove her overcoat. I recognized a few girls from the office with them as well. I thought it nice that they all went out together. It seemed as if they had good friendships outside of work. After a few moments of Dottie strolling in and making a big show of her arrival, she finally recognized me sitting at my booth. She unhooked Jeffrey's arm and skipped over to me so fast you could've sworn it was a magic trick. I caught Jeffrey's reaction as she pulled away. Although I had no interest in Dottie, it gave me a small pleasure in seeing my old boss flinch with jealousy.

"Oh, Henry, dear! What on earth are you doing here?" I stood to greet her as she pecked both of my cheeks. "It's so good to see your cheery face again!"

"It's good to see you too, Dottie. Gotta say I would have never expected to find you in a place like this." She rolled her eyes and took a puff from her long cigarette.

"There you go, Mr. Viefhaus, always making these assumptions about me." She tapped her cigarette twice over the ashtray on my table. "Well, this time, you may be right. Jeffrey's been begging to take me out since you left. I finally gave him a chance to prove himself." I looked past her to see if Jeffrey was still watching. He had ordered two drinks at the bar. I assumed one was for Dottie. And he was making his way over to the table.

"Well, it looks like he's on his way to do that now." Dottie shuttered and grabbed my hand and pulled me toward the dance floor.

"Oh, please don't make me entertain him. Dance with me. Will ya? Just for a little while." I looked over at Jeffrey as he made his way. His expression was clear; I was to stay away from Dottie.

"Gee, Dottie, I don't know. I don't wanna get in the way of anything with you and Jeffrey. He's never much believed that you and I were just friends." She managed to pull me out of my seat and drag me halfway onto the dance floor. She scoffed at me as we skipped passed Jeffrey, only a few feet away now. I gave him a look to show I was sorry, but I knew he would never believe it.

"Oh, Henry, how is anybody as good as you? Don't you want to get back at him? For Pete's sake, the man fired you. Now, c'mon, just one song. I promise. I won't take no for an answer." From that point on, we were dancing. The first song came and went. All the while, Jeffrey's annoyance grew more visible from the sides. I decided to let go. There wasn't anything I could do about Opal tonight, and there wasn't anything I could do about Jeffrey. I knew Dottie had no intention of finding her way back to him. I decided that tomorrow I would go out looking for a job, and then I would write Opal and tell her of my plans to get her away from that Thomas Laverne once and for all.

The night was going splendid. Dottie was a good friend, keeping me sane when all I could do was think about Opal. Of course, I knew that it was only a matter of time before that happiness would end. It seemed lately the joys in my life never stayed long. Something or someone would always drain the small glimmers of hope I had to hold onto. Unfortunately, that someone was the one person I'd hoped it wouldn't be, Dottie.

The music had calmed, and we'd found ourselves drifting back to a table. By this point, Jeffrey had moved on to entertaining two women in the corner of the bar, both eating up everything he said to them. Dottie spotted him and sighed in relief as we sat down at my booth. "Finally. I didn't think that man would ever take the hint." I chuckled but said nothing. She stared at me a while before continuing. "So, have you found work yet?" I took a sip from the Brandy I ordered and shook my head.

"Not yet, but my brother Herman says he may be able to get me a job as a longshoreman. That's what he does. There's good money in that business. You know?" Dottie nodded but said nothing. She seemed different that night, as if there was something she was imagining but couldn't find the words to express it. "Is something on your mind Dottie? You seem dubious."

"Boy, it sure has been awful boring at the office without your shining face around," she grinned, ignoring my question. I nodded and bared my teeth in a polite smile. She stared at me as if she imagined it might be her last day ever seeing me again. "And don't even get me started on our walks to the bus stop, every morning, eight-thirty sharp. Oh, those mornings with you were like an escape." Dottie hugged her arms around her shoulders as she spoke, as if the memories were more comforting than the actual events themselves. I nodded again, unsure of why Dottie was taking us on this trip down memory lane. "I loved all our talks we would have and your frequent stops to the post office. Then we got acquainted with Mr. Milford and started chatting with him on our way. That was, of course, before we learned how much he could talk!" Dottie giggled as she said this, and I laughed with her, thinking back to all the times Milford made us late to the bus stop. “We had to start crossing the street when it came time to pass the post office just to avoid being late.” She sat back in her seat and sighed happily.

I smiled back, happy to look back on good times with a friend. “Going to the post office was practically a religious practice for you. Remember those two weeks you were waiting for a delivery from your father?” My eyes darted up to hers, shocked that she could remember such a detail, one that I’d hoped she’d forgotten about. I suddenly could feel my face reddening at the mere thought of her question. “You made me stop in there every day before and after work before you finally got your package. And to think, all that fuss was over a simple little box.” By now, my face was stiff with embarrassment. I didn’t think Dottie would remember what I picked up from Milford, let alone recalling the size of the packages. “Say, what the devil was even in that box? It was the only one you never opened up right then and there at the post.”

I scratched at the glass of my Brandy and raised it to my lips to take a nervous gulp before answering her. “Gee, I dunno. That was so long ago now.” Dottie sat up and patiently folded her arms across the table as a big smile crept up over her rosy cheeks.

“Oh no, Mr. Viefhaus.” She wagged a perfectly manicured finger at me. “I remember you being completely miserable with anxiety as you waited for that box. I know it had to be somethin’ special. Now let’s have it.” Her eyes beamed as they nearly pierced through me. Why was Dottie all of a sudden so curious about all this? And why was I so shy about tellin’ her the plain truth? “The only time you’re private is when…”

Realization settled on Dottie’s face as she finally understood. She took two long drags from the stem of her cigarette, eyeing me all the while, putting thought into what her next words would be. She tapped the ash into the tray slowly between each puff before she finally spoke again. “Did it have anything to do with that girl back home? What was her name, Jewels? Ruby?”

She snapped her fingers as she tried to remember. “Opal.” I managed to stammer out. I fidgeted with my hands a bit before pulling out a handkerchief to dab the sweat from my palms.

"Well, what is this? Is Henry Viefhaus blushing?" She smiled at me playfully, tickled to see that she had located one of my soft spots. But then, with hardly any transition at all, her face fell into a frown. She was suddenly upset as if I had given her a wrong answer and disappointed her. She took a short puff from her cigarette right before turning her gaze to the table next to us. It seemed she was looking for anywhere to fix her eyes other than on mine. "She's got her hooks in you. Hasn't she?"

I sat up and raised my eyebrows at her. "Pardon?" I said, a little caught off guard. Dottie shook her head and finished the last of her cigarette, only to produce another one in seconds. She quickly lit it and stood from the table.

"I apologize, dear. It seems I may have had too much to drink tonight. I'd better find the others," she said with a deflective tone. I stood and lightly touched her shoulder.

"Should I call a cab for you?" I asked, wondering if she had drank a glass too many. She pulled away from my touch and slowly backed toward her table as a tear fell down her cheek. She must have been as caught off guard as I was by it because she quickly wiped it away and turned toward the door. I had never seen Dottie's sensitive side, and it was clear she was horrified that her emotions had risen to the surface. She backed away slowly, apologizing again with each step.

"No, no. I'll be perfectly fine. Just too much gin for a girl my size. Oh, I hope I haven't ruined your evening."

"Dottie, is something the matter? Have I offended you in some way?" I say, practically chasing after her now. She shook her head and bowed out gracefully.

"No, of course not, Henry. You're the perfect gentleman as always." She forced a polite smile. "Though, I realize now that I've made a complete fool of myself. I'll say goodnight now."

She turned and ran over to Jeffrey. His face went from concern to anger as they exchanged a few words. Then, without hesitation, his eyes darted to me. He pushed by a few neighboring tables until he was standing in front of mine. I stood to be polite, but I knew he wasn't coming to say hello. I wanted to avoid having a harsh conversation. Still, I knew Jeffery would surely jump at any opportunity to pick a fight with me.

"Hello, Jeffrey. I don't quite really know wha-" He put his hand up to silence me. That got my blood boiling faster than I had anticipated.

"No need to explain yourself, Henry. I don't care much for you, if I can be frank. So, I'll make this brief so as not to start an unnecessary quarrel. You would be wise to keep your distance from Dottie." I straightened my tie and gritted my teeth slightly.

"Pardon, but Dottie and I are good friends. I'm sure she's told you this by now."

"No, pardon me, Henry, but I think her interactions with you prove otherwise. There's nothing more despicable than a man who toys with a woman's heart, never once revealing intentions of anything more than free company. There are plenty of men out there far more suitable a choice for a girl like Dottie." I wanted to speak, but I was utterly dumbfounded. Could he honestly suggest that Dottie had feelings for me? Had I been toying with her? I had always assumed Dottie was as much my friend as I was hers.

"Henry! You haven't introduced me to your friend." Herman patted my shoulder as he and Millie joined us. Millie was hanging on his arm now and looked completely smitten with Herman. I turned my glance to Herman, and I could tell by his expression that he hadn't come over to make conversation. He was doing what any brother would have done in this situation, coming to my aide.

"My apologies Herman. This is Jeffrey Warlow from *Edmunds and Company.* He and I used to work together. Jeffrey was my overseer."

Herman snapped his fingers like he had just discovered the light bulb, purposefully avoiding shaking Jeffrey's hand, even after Jeffrey had extended his. "Aha! So, you're the fellow that fired my brother and nearly put him on the streets. Hmm, it's nice to finally put a name with a face. I guess. You'll excuse me if we don't shake hands." Millie giggled as Jeffrey lowered his hand and nodded, straightening his jacket to avoid the awkward silence.

“So, you're the brother, are you? I hope you'll know, as I have explained to Henry, that it was not a personal decision. Just simply following orders.”

“Oh, but of course!” Herman laughed sarcastically. “No respectable man could ever decide that. I would like to think that all the terrible men out there who were following orders had good intentions at heart.” Herman patted Jeffrey’s collar mockingly. “We shouldn’t blame those who follow blindly into battle, just the one giving the orders. Right?”

Jeffrey’s face changed from anger to intimidation as he realized Herman was not there to make friends. “Well, I'm glad to hear you understand.” Jeffrey took a step back, realizing he was now outnumbered. “I guess I'd better move along now.”

“What's the rush? Stay! Have a drink with your new friends. Won’t ya?” I realized then that Herman might have been more drunk than he let on. I put my hand on his shoulder to keep him from following after Jeffrey.

“Maybe next time, Herm. I think Jeffrey has other plans for the evening.” I glared at Jeffrey, and he quickly got the hint. He nodded, understanding exactly what I meant.

“Remember what I said the next time you see Dottie. You’ve done her no good by dangling a carrot.” With those words, Jeffrey turned and headed back to Dottie; they left shortly after. Dottie never once turned back to look at me. Herman and I took a seat at the booth, and Millie sat in his lap. Soon Herman had forgotten all about the matter. I, however, sat quietly for the rest of the night, completely puzzled by what had taken place.

Chapter Six

Henry

"So, what's your experience in the longshoreman business?" asked Robert Ranger, a rather fat man who sat two feet away, puffing on what was left of an old cigar. He was balding, and his suspenders weren't doing too good of a job keeping his pants up over his large belly. He was quite short compared to Herman and me; he couldn't have been taller than five-foot-eight.

It had been three weeks since I moved in with my brother Herman, and still I'd had no news of a prospective job. Finally, Herman heard through a colleague that there might be some openings at his job as a longshoreman. He convinced the boss to give me an interview after buying him two costly cigars.

Herman had coached me on all the right answers to survive an interview with Mr. Ranger before we arrived. Smile, but not too much. Shake hands both before and after the meeting. Don't fidget. Mr. Ranger hates that. It translates to fear. If you're not wearing a tie, you may as well go home. Speak too fast, and he'll think you're not trustworthy. Speak too slowly, and he'll think you were dropped on your head as an infant.

The list seemed to go on. It was exhausting having to recall all of these rules, but I was grateful Herman told them to me. Robert Ranger was definitely a tough shell to crack. I sat up straight and looked him in the eye as we played the interview game in his office, a shabby hole-in-the-wall just a mile from the docks.

"None, Sir," I finally reply to his question, "but I'm a fast learner. I can guarantee you that."

"Mmm." That was all he gave me. I couldn't tell if it was a disappointed interjection or a satisfied one. "What's your background, son?" He pulled out today's paper and straightened it out on his desk, altogether avoiding my eyes like he didn't care if I interviewed at all.

"Oh, I've done all sorts of work, mostly manual labor, Sir. Back home, I did a lot of farming with my Pa. I know a little in mechanics as well. Most recently, I was a desk clerk at *Edmunds and Company*." Mr. Ranger's eyes perked up, and for the first time, he met my gaze.

"You worked at *Edmunds and Company*? How long?"

"Just a little under a year, Sir. I got let go mid-December of last year."

"Oh! You must be acquainted with my daughter then!" My heart sank, as I could almost hear Dottie's name rolling around in his mind, ready to be spoken. Was this man Dottie's father? It made my stomach churn at the mere thought of the awkward night we shared only weeks ago at that underground club.

Dottie's last name wasn't Ranger. It was Gold, but I recalled her saying that she was married for a short time when she was eighteen. The marriage only lasted four months. According to Dottie, they had the marriage annulled after she caught him in the act of adultery.

"Y-your daughter works at Edmunds?"

"Sure does! Small world and all, you knowin' my Cathy." Relief hit as soon as I recalled Catherine Ranger. She was the front desk secretary, the very first face you saw when walking into the office. She was rather chubby, like her father, but the sweetest woman, nonetheless. She was in her early thirties and well past the desirable time to find a mate. But she always smiled anyway, never letting on that she may be growing more and more lonely as the months passed by.

"Oh yes, of course, Sir! How could I forget a woman as lovely as she? Cathy is simply swell!" Mr. Ranger beamed with pride as we spoke about his daughter. The interview shifted from what I knew about hard work to what I knew about Cathy. I didn't mind it much myself. I was beginning to grow weary that I wouldn't get the job up until I mentioned Edmund's and Company. It seemed my knowing Cathy had sealed my fate, and in that moment, I was grateful for her acquaintance. After what seemed like mere seconds of chatting it up about the good old days at Edmund's, Mr. Ranger finally got serious.

"Alright, so I'll give you the facts," he said, giving me a serious tone. "I like ya kid. You seem smart." I sat up straight and folded my hands in my lap, appreciative of the compliment.

"Thank you, Sir," I said eagerly. But Mr. Ranger quickly put his hand up to silence me.

"Let me finish. You seem smart, and your brother Herman here does good work. Seeing as how you come from the same background, I can only assume you'll work just as hard." He inhaled a drag from his cigar and glanced down at the paperwork again shaking his head all the while. "The only problem is we've got too many men right now. We're supposed to be cutting back, but I've been fighting it. The facts are when summer comes 'round, I know we're gonna get slammed. We'll need the extra help."

I nodded my head understanding but not really sure what would come next. "Chances are," Mr. Ranger continued, "upper management is gonna have a field day if they learn I've hired a new hand. But I was pleased to hear all about your friendship with my girl Cathy, and it softened my heart towards you, Henry. It made me realize that maybe you and I could be friends." He looked at me with pleading eyes, as if I was now in charge of whether or not the job would be mine.

"Pardon, Sir, but I'm not sure we're understanding," Herman interrupted as he rolled up the sleeves on his uniform.

"Has Henry got the job, or hasn't he?" Mr. Ranger sat up in his chair, allowing his belly to tuck in some from behind the desk.

"Well, I guess there is no easy way to suggest this, so I'm just gonna come right out with it." He sighed as he puffed on his saliva-soaked cigar. I tapped my fingers against my knee. I knew Herman advised against fidgeting, but at this point, I couldn't help it. "I want you to take my daughter out." My eyes widened, and my heart sank as I tried to process his unnerving request. "You seem to be quite the dashing young fellow. I believe it could only have been a helping hand from God that you would come here looking for work just after being in the same office as my Cathy. Cathy's a lovely girl. She's just never been much of a looker," he said with a look of guilt. I shifted in my chair and gulped, too scared to openly agree with him. "Perhaps you could-" he struggled for the right words to say, "entertain her for me. You know. Make her feel special is all I'm asking. If you do that, I'll hire you right here on the spot."

Herman and I exchanged a look, unsure if this deal was even worth the job. I needed work, but did I need it that bad? And what about Opal? Herman sighed but said nothing. The decision was mine alone to make.

"Sir, I must confess to you, I'm sort of involved with a girl back home. I was planning on sending for her to come down to California to be with me very soon." Mr. Ranger's face became grave as he tapped the remaining ashes from his cigar into a tray that sat on his desk.

"Are the two of you engaged, son?" he asked, annoyed. I shook my head at him, angry with myself that I couldn't yet say otherwise. "Well then, it's settled! You take my Cathy out to a nice, fancy restaurant and make her feel like she's the prettiest girl you know. Hell, I'll even pay for it!" I squirmed in my chair, wanting so badly to tell him no and bolt for the door. "Look son, I'm not asking you to marry her. I'm not even asking you to like her. Just take her out for one night. Give her a little attention, so she can gain some damn confidence. I just want my Cathy to get some assurance about herself, so she can get out there and find herself a decent husband. Her mother and I can tell her all day long that she's beautiful, but sometimes it just ain't enough.

She's pushing thirty-one, ya know. My poor girl is running out of time."

Mr. Ranger's face was all but one flinch away from an everlasting shameful frown. I suddenly felt sorrow for the poor gent; he was just a helpless father trying to do right by his daughter. I exhaled as I could feel myself finally giving in. I envisioned Cathy in my mind. She was a rather plain woman, not nearly as beautiful as Opal. I would never have approached her otherwise, but I suppose every woman ought to feel desirable from time to time. "Oh, alright. I suppose I could do this for you just this one time. After all, Cathy was very kind to me while I was employed at Edmunds. You're sure it would just be this once?"

"Of course, my boy! I wouldn't want to obligate you any further than that." He stood to his feet with a wide grin across his face and extended his palm to mine. "So, do we have a deal?" he asked, confident of my response.

I looked at Herman with apprehension. Sadly, Herman gave me no response in return. I looked back at Mr. Ranger. I realized he was my only option in getting Opal to California as soon as possible.

"Yes, Sir," I said begrudgingly, though my face had a smile as wide as the ocean. Mr. Ranger smiled back with content.

"Henry, welcome to the longshoreman business. You'll start Wednesday." Herman and I stood as we shook hands with Mr. Ranger and quickly left his office. Mr. Ranger didn't follow. Instead, he began making phone calls and yelling into the receiver. He was back to his managerial tasks without a moment's rest. Once outside and out of earshot, Herman finally spoke up.

"You really gonna take that girl out?" I nodded with frustration and withdrew my pipe from my inner pocket.

"Well, it doesn't look like I've got much of a choice on the matter now, does it? I need work with good wages. This may be as good as it gets for a fellow like me."

"Well, what about Opal?"

"Nothing's changed," I answered, angry that Herman, of all people, would actually question my loyalties to her. "I'll see to it that Mr. Ranger knows that I'm a hard worker and keeps me around long after his worries for his daughter, Cathy, have subsided. I'll save up and send for Opal by year's end. I guarantee."

"You gonna tell her?"

"What's to tell at this point? Who's to say this imaginary date will even take place?"

"Well, supposin' it does? Will you tell her?" I rolled my eyes at Herman's sudden need for answers about all this. The truth of the matter was I needed money, money that I could save up and eventually buy a train ticket to send for Opal. I was going to do it by any means necessary. I'm sure Opal could understand that. I ignored Herman's question and walked him back to his workstation on the dock.

"I'm sorry. I just don't feel much like talking about this. I'll see you at home, Herm," I said, taking a turn and heading for home. Herman nodded and returned to his work. I walked to a bus stop about a mile away from the docks and smoked my pipe in silence. All I could think about were the terrible messes I kept getting myself into, first with Dottie and now this dreadful deal with Cathy's father. What would Opal think of me? I didn't want to find out.

The bus ride into town was a quiet one. Not many people rode it during the middle of the day. Most folks were off at work during this hour. The bus went over a dip and bounced all of the passengers about half a foot above their seats. A woman and her two children sitting in the front of the bus laughed amongst themselves at the surprise of it. I smiled at them as they reminded me of the time I took Opal to the county fair back in St. Louis. She had never been, and it was our first official date.

The ride on the bus that day was also very bumpy. It seemed like we were going over a dip every other second. At first, Opal was trying to contain her poise. I was doing my best to hold her upright while we bounced along, but it was no use. Our bus was no match for that dirt road into the countryside. It wasn't long before the two of us were laughing so obnoxiously that an elderly woman had to remind us to mind our manners while on public transit. Opal and I couldn't help it. All our efforts to impress one another went flying out of the window the moment we realized this bus would spare us no mercy to remain proper. It was one of our most memorable days spent together. I missed her now more than ever. It pained me to be so far from her. But it also inspired me to work hard, so I could afford to give her a life and a decent one at that.

Once in town, I noticed we were approaching the post office. I suddenly felt an urgency to write Opal. That memory of her had me feeling especially romantic, and I needed to tell her I was working hard to get her to California. I pulled down on the bell cord and felt the bus slow as we approached the next stop. I quickly stepped out and hurried down the street to the post office. *San Pedro Post Office* was painted neatly above the doors. The bells dangling from the doorknob jingled as I entered to greet Milford. He was sitting behind the counter, high on a stool with a pipe resting between his teeth and today's paper in his hand. His glasses rested at the bridge of his nose, and his chubby cheeks were as rosy as ever. If it weren't for the fact that he was missing a beard, someone could have easily mistaken him for St. Nick himself. What was left of the hair on his head was a silvery-white, and his mustache was perfectly twisted up at the ends.

"Well, if it isn't Henry Viefhaus! How ya doin,' Son? It's been a while." He stood up and folded his paper in half to greet me. He was as cheery as ever. It felt good to see a familiar face.

"Hello, Milford." I smiled. "It's good to see you." Milford tapped his chin and looked up toward the ceiling.

"Well, I don't recall getting anything in for you. You waitin' on a package?"

"No, Sir." I shook my head at him and smiled. "Not this time. I was hoping to send out a letter today. Have you got any paper?"

"Of course, Mr. Viefhaus. I'll be right back." I nodded politely while Milford disappeared into the back room. He was back in record timing. I thanked him and found space on a nearby counter to write.

San Pedro CA
Feb 24, 1928

Dearest Girlie,

It is rather early this morning to write, but I'm not yet working. So, dear, I have time until Monday to write to you. I've finally found work! I'm going to be a longshoreman alongside my brother, Herman, which means you and I are one step closer to being together.

But now is when my thoughts are whole upon you, my dear, so now please endure my letter. I'm glad to get the chance to send my sweetie a few lines and give you my thoughts. You, baby mine, give me courage to work. I work for us. For us, I will be. I'm sure. For sweet woman, you cannot change your mind. For I love you, dear one, and must someday have you for my own, all my own. Won't that be great, just you and I all alone to love? And I can build our future. Of course, dear, all clouds cannot have a silver lining, but I'm sure enthused and pleased over the chance for my prospective bride.

Sweetheart, you don't realize just how enthused I am all the time, over my one desire - you. Honey, how I'll enjoy your love, your kisses, company and all that goes with married life. No one can know the sincerity of my love for you. Sweet girl, I wish it were not so cold there, for I don't want you to suffer from cold. But soon I will send for you, and San Pedro is a much warmer town. I cannot wait to have you by my side again, sweet Opal. Well, baby doll, I'll sign off for today. Good-bye, dear. I love you dearly.

Yours,

Henry

I bent the letter into a trifold and sealed it in an available envelope on the counter. I walked over to Milford, who waited patiently for me. "All set, Mr. Viefhaus?" I nodded and handed the letter to him. "Alright, that'll be five cents for the stamp." I dug through my pockets for loose change and handed him a nickel just as the bells on the entrance door jingled. I looked over to find Dottie standing in the doorway holding a cigarette holder to her lips. When our eyes met, her face turned a pale white, almost like she had just seen a ghost. I turned to Milford and thanked him as I collected my things, not sure if acknowledging the awkward tension would make things worse. Before I had time to decide, Dottie marched right over to the counter and placed a letter in Milford's hand. It was already stamped and sealed.

"Hello, Milford, dear. I need to send this letter out. Can I pay you for express mail?" Milford nodded and put the letter in a designated bin behind him.

"Of course, Ms. Gold. Anything else I can do for you today?" She shook her head at Milford and picked through her coin purse after he gave her the price. Without looking up, she finally spoke to me. "Hello, Henry. It's a surprise seeing you here."

I wondered how it was a surprise to her. I came to this exact post office almost three times a week when we used to work together. I ignored the idea and replied nonetheless. "Dottie. I would have to say the same thing to you. I suppose. Shouldn't you be in the office?" She took a puff from her cigarette holder and blew it away from my direction.

"Not today. I wasn't feeling too well on account of my night. Jeffrey took me out again, and I suppose I had too much to drink." Both of us fell silent as we realized an enormous elephant had just entered the post office. I could only imagine we were both silently reliving the nightmare from three weeks ago when she burst into tears and fled the speakeasy. I pretended I didn't remember the memory and nodded. I still hadn't fully grasped what had happened. Dottie shook her head and took in a deep breath, finally willing herself to look at me. "Henry, dear, could I have a word with you privately, outside?" I could feel Milford's stares at the two of us. I suppose he must have wondered if there was ever anything between the two of us. I thanked Milford for his help, and Dottie did the same. We stepped outside and walked along the sidewalk, passing all the small shops we'd passed so many times on our way to work together. Dottie finished off her cigarette and pulled out another one attaching it to her long turquoise holder while we walked. She still hadn't said a word, and I was beginning to grow impatient. I stopped walking and turned to look at her.

"Dottie, what's this about? If you think you owe me an apology for the other night, I can assure you it isn't necessary." She took a fresh puff from her new cigarette and patted my shoulder.

"Oh, Henry. I fear I've made a complete fool of myself. I should never have run off the way I did. And I should never have spoken to Jeffrey. I didn't know he'd go and address you about it."

"Pardon me, Dottie. But I still haven't the slightest idea of what I even said to upset you. Why did you run away?" I could see water beginning to well in Dottie's eyes, but she fought hard to keep it from forming into tears. She shook her head at me and tapped her foot on the pavement.

"I'm not all the way sure, to be honest. One minute I'm prying about that girl of yours from back home-" she exhaled deeply, "and the next, I'm an emotional wreck. Can you ever forgive me for how I acted?"

It seemed a small realization was settling into both of our minds. I looked at Dottie and squeezed her arm with assurance. "Now, now. There isn't any reason to cry. Of course, I can forgive you." She nodded her head at me, thankful to have won my friendship. "Dottie, I need to ask you one question. You need to promise you'll answer truthfully and forthright." She nodded in agreement and gave me as much eye contact as she could for someone who had just begged for forgiveness, seemingly over nothing.

"What is it, Henry?"

"Have you grown feelings for me?" A look of horror returned to her eyes, the same look that plagued her face just minutes before when she had spotted me in the post office. After the shock of the question had subsided, she answered honestly, as I'd requested. The problem was that it wasn't the answer I was hoping for.

“Yes,” she nodded. “I can’t help but wonder if you might have feelings for me as well,” she said with raised eyebrows and stepping closer toward me. Before I knew what was happening, she was leaning in as if she were about to kiss me!

Chapter Seven

Opal

"Well, try it on, sweetheart." Thomas was beaming from ear to ear, absolutely pleased with himself over the pearl bracelet he had purchased for me. He had taken me out to lunch at a nice restaurant right in the heart of town in hopes to impress me. We sat outside on the patio at a table that had been beautifully decorated with a lace tablecloth and fresh flowers. Poor Thomas was trying as hard as he possibly could to win me over. I still hadn't given him a proper yes to his proposal for marriage, and with Henry almost at my grasp, I hardly had any intention to. But to Mama, Thomas was our safety net, and I didn't want to disappoint her. So, I entertained Thomas whenever she requested to keep her happy.

I picked up the bracelet from its smooth, black velvety case and unlatched the hook. Thomas reached for my new bracelet and helped me clasp the pearly beauty around my wrist. It really was a beautiful piece of jewelry. It must have cost him a fortune. I held it up to the sunlight to get a better look. The pearls looked so elegant on my arm, and I felt like a true lady.

"Do you like it, dear?" He pried humbly awaiting my praise report.

"Oh, Henry, it's more beautiful than I could have ever imagined. Thank you, darling. It's absolutely wonderful!" I beamed. Thomas smiled curtly, but I could tell something had displeased him. "Is something the matter?"

He withdrew his handkerchief from his pocket and dabbed at the few beads of sweat that had formed on his forehead. He shook his head and looked down at the table. "Well, you just- you just called me Henry." Fear set in on my face as I quickly realized my terrible mistake. I brought my hand to my mouth in complete horror but said nothing. All I could do was stare at him, eyes wide. "Is this Henry fellow always going to be a source of comfort for you?"

"Thomas, I'm completely mortified. Please forgive me, dear. It was merely a slip of the tongue. I can assure you." He waved his hand at my apology and feigned a smile.

"It's quite alright, Opal. I know the two of you had quite the history before he moved away." I nodded humbly, hoping he could talk himself out of his own doubt.

"Thank you for understanding, dear. I can promise you I will not make the same mistake twice." He played with a spoon on the table and nodded slightly. After a moment's pause, he withdrew a two-dollar bill from his pocket and placed it on the table.

"Right. Well, we'd better get going. I've got a doctor's visit this afternoon with the Walsh family." I nodded and collected my things. I knew the embarrassment of my slip would not wear off so easy. Thomas and Henry had never been much of friends before; it seemed they all but despised one another. I remember their first time meeting each other. In fact, it was the same day I had met Henry.

Right after Henry had swept me off my feet at Mr. Penny's shoe store, though we barely knew each other. I hoped he would show up to the soldier's appreciation ball as he promised. Henry did show up like he'd promised, and that night was one of the best nights I'd ever had. The St. Louis City Hall had been beautifully decorated, and the food was absolutely delicious. Mama had paid three dollars for my ticket in the door that night, which was not easy for a family like us. Mama said the sacrifice was worth it if I found myself a decent man to marry.

I wore the shoes that Mama and I had picked out earlier that day at Mr. Penny's store, along with my nicest blue dress. It was a cocktail dress with hand-sewn sequins and thin threads of fringe sewn to the bottom. My best friend Laura and I attended the ball together that night. Laura was timid compared to me, which wasn't saying much, so I took over the responsibility of controlling all of our conversations that night.

Laura and I danced with a few decent suitors, but none of which we were very interested in. All of the men seemed to have one tiny flaw that made Laura and I cringe. One gentleman, while very friendly, had been the most talkative spirit we had ever encountered. Lieutenant Greer was his name, and I remember eyeing Laura the entire time, hoping that she would catch my cries for help. I should have known Laura would not be much help, as she was not the type of girl to assert herself in an uncomfortable situation. Lieutenant Greer was a tall, hefty fellow, and he talked about everything from fishing to the Great War. Every time he said a word that started with the letter P or T, a little bit of saliva would fly out from his pursed lips, and I would have to lean my head to the side to avoid getting spat on. That's when I met Thomas.

Thomas was by far the most dashing fellow at the dinner that evening. He had flirted with several women at the ball, and it seemed like he just knew how to captivate a lady's attention. I overheard several conversations of other girls saying that they hoped Thomas would approach them. I, however, had no interest in him as I was still patiently awaiting the mysterious Henry, hoping that he would soon arrive.

Thomas walked right up to Lieutenant Greer and me. He showed no interest in letting the soldier finish even his last sentence to me.

"Pardon me, but I couldn't help but notice you from my table." Lieutenant Greer seemed entirely baffled by Thomas' rude interruption, but I couldn't help but giggle just a little. "Would you care to dance?" Thankful to get away from the Lieutenant and his incessant babbling, I hooked arms with

Thomas and headed for the dance floor without so much as a nod to Greer.

Once we joined the other courting couples on the platform, I let out a relieved sigh. "Thank you. I didn't know how I was going to escape that man."

"Oh, it's no trouble. You looked like you needed a helping hand. I'm surprised your girlfriend didn't rescue you first," he laughed. I chuckled as I rested my hand on his shoulder, and we swayed to the light jazz.

"Oh, poor Laura. She's more shy than a cat around a dog." We both laughed, and our eyes rested on one another's. For a short moment, I thought I might be taken with Thomas. He was the first fellow I'd met who didn't have some odd tick.

"Well, she doesn't seem to be so shy around that gentleman over there." Thomas pointed with his eyes to a gentleman that had gotten Laura's attention. She was laughing in the corner and covering her face with her dainty hands. The man who had caught her attention was Laura's current fiancé, Ray Carter.

"Well, would ya look at that? I guess Laura had it in her after all," I said, looking back at Thomas and smiling. I glanced down at his suit. He was one of the few gentlemen not wearing a uniform, just a beige suit jacket and matching pants.

"I can't help but notice you're not in uniform, soldier. Are you above the dress requirements?"

Thomas shook his head at me as we continued to square-step. "That's because I'm not a soldier, ma'am. I'm a doctor. I was granted permission to attend on account of my many house calls to the base here in St. Louis. Sometimes the doctors inside want second opinions."

"Ah, so you're a doctor. It's no wonder you knew I needed saving." Thomas and I giggled at each other. I was beginning to forget about Henry. In fact, at this point, I barely missed him. I had only had one encounter with him, and the memory of that was slowly fading. It was right when I felt the most comfortable with Thomas that Henry's face appeared. I didn't notice him until he was halfway on the dance floor and headed straight toward Thomas and me. He looked out of breath, but very determined nonetheless.

"There you are, darling. I hoped you'd still be here. I apologize for the delay." My eyes lit up involuntarily, and I could feel my face flush to red. Thomas didn't release his grip from around my waist, but I pulled my arms from his shoulders and held them close to my chest. Henry looked so dashing. I could barely contain my gaze at his broad shoulders and charming grin. Henry extended his hand to mine and bowed slightly. "Shall we?"

Thomas looked at me to see my reaction but did not allow time for my response. "I beg your pardon, Sir, but the young lady and I are in the middle of a dance. You'll have to wait your turn."

Henry let out a confident chuckle without so much as even acknowledging Thomas with a courtesy glance. His eyes stayed rested on mine. "I'll ask again, Opal. Shall we?" I could feel the heat coming off of Thomas as his chest began to rise and fall more quickly. I had no idea what the right decision was in that moment. I was waiting for Henry all night, but Thomas was the one who had calmed my nerves. I was much more interested in Henry, but Thomas approached me first.

My mother's words rang in my head. *Above all else, follow your first mind.* She had been trying to bestow some motherly wisdom on Laura and me before we left that evening. At that moment, an overwhelming feeling to take Henry's hand took over my senses. I suddenly had a familiar and warm feeling in my heart toward Henry, and I knew that if I didn't go with him, I'd inevitably regret it.

I reached for Henry's hand after what felt like hours of waiting. Thomas' face was more surprised than I had anticipated. "Do forgive me, Thomas, but Henry was my date this evening. I-it was wonderful to dance with you tonight. Thank you again for saving me from that talkative Lieutenant Greer. You really are a lifesaver." I forced out a laugh to lighten the mood. Thomas nodded at me but only out of an obligation to be polite. He didn't say another word, only walked away without so much as a whisper. I immediately felt guilty, but I was still happy that I had chosen to go with Henry.

Henry and I laughed and danced for the next hour. I had never been so taken with a man. Henry didn't wear a uniform either that night. I assumed he was an invited guest like Thomas was. We were sitting at a table in the corner of the hall. Henry nursed a Brandy while I sipped on wine. "So tell me, are you a doctor as well? You're one of the few men in here without a uniform on." Henry raised his eyebrows at me with questioning eyes.

"As well? I thought this was a soldier's ball. Who in here is a doctor?"

"Thomas is, the gentleman I was dancing with before you arrived." Henry scoffed at the mention of Thomas.

"Please don't spoil the night with the mention of that intolerable prude. You're lucky I got there when I did, or he'd have proposed within the hour." I giggled softly at his need to puff out his chest in front of me. "No, no, no. I'm a man that likes to work with his hands. Machine mechanics is more of my specialty."

"Well then, how did you get in here? Were you invited?" I could sense a hint of jealousy in my voice. I hoped Henry hadn't received an invitation from another woman. He leaned in close to me with a smirk.

"Well, to be honest, I wanted to see you so much, I snuck in. I followed in behind one of the chefs in the back." I covered my mouth with my hand to keep from smiling so big.

"Henry, you could get in a lot of trouble!"

"I know, but I couldn't wait to see you again. I didn't know how else to find you." His eyes were genuine as they met mine, and all at once, I could feel a burning in my chest. It was a strange feeling for me, but I knew it was a good one.

I was right. No sooner had I mentioned the trouble he could get into, did a cluster of four tall men, all but one in uniform, approached the table that Henry and I sat. Thomas was among them with a look of vengeance in his eyes. One of the tall men nodded at me and quickly turned his gaze to Henry.

"How'd you get in here, boy?"

I felt the sudden flush of red again set on my face. Henry didn't seem to be even slightly phased by the man's blatant demeaning attitude. "I walked right in, same as you."

The man sighed and rested his hand on his belt. "You know this is a private event for soldiers and invited guests only?"

"Yes, Sir. I am aware. How do you suppose I was informed of this event?" Henry's sarcasm was beginning to annoy the tall man.

"You need to leave. Now."

"Is that so? And how do you figure?" Henry scoffed. The tall man leaned right into Henry's face and spoke slowly.

"You ain't a soldier. And you for damn sure ain't invited." I looked over at Thomas, who had been quiet up to this point. I shot him a mean look. I knew it was him that had brought attention to Henry's attendance. Thomas quickly looked away and took a sip from his glass of whiskey. Henry turned his gaze back to me and continued with the conversation as if no one was there.

"So, Opal. Where can I find you? Are you close by?"

"That's it. I'm done talking." The tall soldier's patience had worn out. He grabbed Henry by the shoulders and forced him to stand up. A second soldier stepped in and grabbed Henry's arm to keep him from fighting back.

"Whoa, easy, fellas! Can't I entertain the young lady in peace?" The soldiers didn't answer him. Instead, they began to escort him by force from the table and toward the town hall exit. "Don't worry, Opal!" He called out to me as they practically dragged him. "I'll find you again!" This time I knew that my cheeks had turned an impossible shade of bright red. I looked around the ballroom to find everyone staring at the commotion of Henry's grand exit. Their stares quickly turned to me as they began to whisper amongst themselves. Thomas stayed behind as the soldiers did his dirty work. He placed his hand on my shoulder, aware of my discomfort in all this.

"Opal, dear, are you alright?" I batted his hand away and quickly headed for the ladies' room, too mortified and angry to speak. Even in all my anger, I began to feel more certain of Henry the longer the night went on. I knew someday I would marry that unapologetic and carefree man. I had to.

"Hold on a minute, Opal. I would like to discuss something with you." Thomas' still tone brought me out of my daydream, and suddenly I was back at the table with the beautiful pearly bracelet hugged around my wrist. I hated that he was my reality now. I wanted to be rid of him.

I sat up in my chair and eyed him very carefully, unsure of the words to come. "Yes, Thomas?"

He toyed with his handkerchief a while longer before mustering up enough courage to speak. "I've had suspicions for a while now that you've had little interest in starting a future with me." I shook my head, guilty as could be.

"Oh, Thomas, don't say that. I'm only—"

"No need to explain yourself, Opal. I'm not angry with you. I would simply like for us to be comfortable enough to say what's in our hearts without passing judgment. Do you think you can promise me that, Opal?" I nodded, but in my heart, I wasn't sure if I even believed myself. Thomas reached for my hand across the table and held it gently in his palms. "You know I want nothing more than to marry you. But frankly, I can't wait around forever for your answer. I know that I can never be the man you loved, but I know I can make you happy. If you give me an honest chance, I'm sure that love will come." I sighed as tears formed in my eyes without permission.

"Oh, Thomas."

"Please. All I'm asking is that you open up your heart long enough to let me in. You may love Henry now, but in due time, you'll see that I am the right choice." Each word stung me more deeply than the one before. Lately, it didn't feel like I had much of a choice at all. I didn't want to think about life without Henry. But he was there, and I was here. "I can provide for you, Opal. I can provide for your entire family. Your sweet mother would never have to work again, nor your sisters. With you by my side, as my wife, I would never let you even so much as lift a finger."

Considering Thomas' offer was one of the most adult and painful decisions I had been asked to make in my eighteen years on earth. Yet, somehow, I found myself imagining the possibility of a life with him. The perks to being a doctor's wife would be plenty, and I liked the idea of Mama not having to strain her back in the garden behind the house. I knew a life with Henry would be much more strenuous in the beginning. He had only just found work, and he'd have to work his way up from the bottom.

"I want to take care of you, Opal Pleasant. I know you love him, but he cannot provide for you the way I can. You're a woman now, and you've got more than yourself to think about, dear. Consider my proposal, seriously this time. Tell me that you will."

I nodded at Thomas quietly as tears stained the tablecloth. "You're right, Thomas. I have not been honest with you." He handed me his handkerchief, and I dabbed away my tears, careful not to smudge my makeup. "I will consider your offer." Thomas stood from the table and pushed in his chair.

"Good."

"But I can't make you any promises, Thomas." As soon as I uttered the words, I regretted them. Tears came streaming down again as I tried my best to act like a woman. Thomas straightened his jacket and nodded curtly at me.

"We can discuss this once more if you like, but I can't waste too much more time on this. I'm sorry if that's too frank, but you must understand the position you've put me in. I'm more than ten years your senior, Opal. My family is putting a lot of pressure on this matter. I need to marry quickly." I understood what he meant and nodded through more tears. He spared no more sympathy for my pain. "I have to get back to work now. I'll see you later in the week. Good day, Opal." With those last few cold words, he was gone, without so much as even a glance at me before he left.

I decided to walk home, so I could have more time to think. I considered Thomas' words. How could I ever be happy with a man I didn't care for? It wouldn't be right of me to put that sort of burden on myself nor would it be fair to Thomas. I strolled along the sidewalks through downtown St. Louis. The sun was bright as it hung in the sky that day. I looked around at all the people out; it seemed everyone was having a wonderful day except for me. At that moment, I hated Thomas. I hated him for forcing me to make a decision like this, love or stability. What girl my age should be burdened to decide such a thing? How could Thomas put me in such an awful position? Of course, I knew the easy decision was Henry; that was the decision I wanted to make. I decided at that moment that Henry was the man I would marry, no matter what happened.

You're a selfish girl. The thought crept into my mind before I even got the chance to refute it. As much as I wanted to deny it, there was one truth that Thomas said earlier that I couldn't ignore. I had more than just myself to consider. Mama's been begging me to marry Thomas, not only because she likes him, but because she desperately needs a break. Mama works so hard for the twins and me. It'd be a shame to marry Henry, only to learn that we couldn't support them. Mama would be devastated. I wiped away a tear as I stomped down the street. But I loved Henry! I couldn't imagine a life apart from him, and I dared anyone who would make me try.

My heels knocked against the concrete as I made my way to the outskirts of town and toward home. I walked past the library and the post office across the street. I was tempted to run over and write Henry another letter, but I knew it wouldn't be fair to Thomas if I didn't give his proposal some serious thought. I strolled out of town with my hands tightly curled in the pockets of my overcoat and trotted the rest of the way.

Mama and the girls were in the garden out back when I arrived home. The twins were bubbling with laughter as always. I could hear them playing while Mama scolded them every few minutes about their lack of diligence.

"Girls! Pay attention to your work. Soon you'll be working this garden all by yourselves." Mama's distant words haunted me as I quickly ran inside the house before they noticed I was back from my lunch with Thomas. I headed straight toward my room in desperate need of isolation.

I hated that garden. I hated everything it represented. Mama had worked her hands raw long before the twins were born just to get by. I thought back to the first time I realized we were poor. I was seven years old. I was helping my papa harvest some carrots out back when Mama came out to fuss at us.

"Opal," Mama said with a firm voice. She was bouncing Nettie, who was but a toddler, on her hip and tying an apron around her waist at the same time. "You be sure and pull those carrots just like your daddy does, by the base and straight up."

"Yes, Mama," I said.

"And be sure and check the width before you pull one. Mrs. Nelson likes her carrots full grown. You hear?" Mama continued.

"Honey, leave her be. She's doing a fine job," Papa finally cut in, never once drawing his eyes away from the soil.

"I'm sure she is, but we can't be too careful, dear. This is our only harvest for the next month." Mama argued.

"Yes, but we need not fret in front of the girls." Daddy said calmly, smiling at Mama like doing so would melt all her worries away. In a way, it seemed to work. But the peace was short-lived as the reality of our lives began to settle in.

"We've got a long winter ahead of us," Mama finally said, this time with a softness in her voice that only Papa could provoke. "I've sold just about every dress I own, and the land back here just doesn't seem to be as fertile as it was when we first bought this place." Tears welled in Mama's eyes. The sight of Mama crying made my stomach churn.

"I know, dear," Papa said rising to his feet to come to her aid. He sighed as he held her. "We've got God and each other. We're going to be alright. I promise," he said, turning his gaze to give me an assuring wink. Though they were careful to hide it, I knew as I watched my parents that only worse conditions were yet to come for our family. And it scared me.

I forced myself to banish that terrible memory out of my thoughts. Instead, I laid in my bed and allowed my imagination to run wild. Henry and Thomas raced back and forth in my mind. I was suddenly jealous of my best friend, Laura. She didn't have to make any difficult decisions when it came to marriage. Laura's parents were well off, so she didn't have anyone that depended on her. Laura also had older siblings that would take on that responsibility long before she would have to.

I sat up and walked over to my vanity in the corner of my room. I pulled the drawer out and picked out Henry's most recent letter to me. It was kind and sweet, but my heart broke as I read over his words again. I could sense how troubled for money Henry was as I read carefully. All the saving and planning he had to do just to buy my train ticket brought me grief. I despised how often money was in the midst of my love life. I stood up from my desk and quickly walked down the stairs and headed toward the front door. I passed Mama in the hall as I strolled confidently toward the front door.

"Ah, Opal, you're back. How was your lunch with Thomas?" I brushed past her and curled my hands in my coat pocket.

"I'll be back soon, Mama." I ignored her question and quickly fled out the door before she could scold me. I skipped back into town. It only took me about fifteen minutes on account of how quickly I moved. Usually, a walk into town would take nearly a half-hour, but today I was on a mission. I liked that we weren't more inland. Our distance from town seemed perfect. A ten-minute journey by car and a twenty-five-minute walk, not too close and not too far.

I found my way to the post office and pried open the door to find the short little man from weeks ago sitting behind the desk and reading a newspaper. His glasses sat at the bridge of his nose, and he looked up at me only slightly when I entered.

"Well, look who it is! Good day to you, Miss. Long-time-no-see." I smiled brightly at him, happy to see a cheery face for the first time that day.

"Yes, good day. What was your name, Sir?"

"Leroy! Leroy Pepperman."

"Leroy. What a nice name. I figured I may as well learn your name since I have a feeling I'm going to be dropping in an awful lot. I'm Opal."

"Yes, I remember you, Miss Pleasant. I recall your name from the letter you wrote a few weeks ago." Leroy tucked some of his leftover shirt into his waistband and folded his newspaper in half. "So, what brings you in today?"

"I need to mail out a letter. I'll probably be mailing out letters more often from here on out."

"Since you're going to be dropping by more frequently, perhaps I can interest you in renting a box."

"A post office box? I've never considered renting one before."

"Well, it sure would make your life a lot simpler if you did." I imagined myself making trips to the post office to drop off and receive secret letters from Henry in my mysterious box. It all seemed so adventurous and alluring.

"How much to rent one?"

"Twenty cents a month. And lucky for you, we've just had an opening."

"Really, which one?"

Leroy pulled out a clipboard with a list of box numbers on it. He ran his pointer finger down the page until he landed on a line. "Eh, lemme see here. Ah, here we are, box 175." He looked up at me anticipating my answer. I bit my lip for a moment, wondering to myself if this meant that I was silently choosing Henry by getting a box solely dedicated to writing him. I let out a hopeful sigh and smiled at the nice, little man.

"I'll take it!"

Chapter Eight

Henry

"Damn thing. I can never get it right on the first go." I stood inches from the front door mirror fidgeting with my tie. My father had taught me plenty of times how to tie a simple knot. Still, every time I attempted it by myself, it came out uneven with the tailpiece hanging much longer than the blade. Without announcement, Herman was suddenly in my view in the reflection with a wide grin across his face and snickering. I shook my head at him and tried the knot again. "Do I amuse you, Herman?" Herman let out a boisterous laugh that could have only derived from the enjoyment of seeing my pain.

"I'm sorry, Henry. I can't help myself!" He shook his head at me in disbelief and pity. "I mean boy, he really got you! I never thought this would actually happen, but here we are!" Herman let out another hearty laugh and walked away shaking his head all the way into the kitchen.

"You're surprised? I'm the one that's got to go through with it." I finished tying a decent knot. I followed Herman into the kitchen where he picked out a nice apple for himself and adjourned to the living room to stretch out on the sofa. "Mr. Ranger's got some nerve putting me in this position. Has he no decency. I mean, I'm practically engaged to another woman! If I didn't need the money, I'da quit by now." Herman took a bite out of the crisp apple as I followed suit into the living room.

"Well, don't get all emotional now. You need this job if you're ever gonna get Opal down here, so you can propose for real. Who knows? You might enjoy yourself tonight." I shook my head in disbelief.

"I doubt that. I mean, Cathy's swell, but she's a woman in her thirties. I won't even be twenty-two for another few months. What will there even be to talk about tonight? We haven't worked together in months now."

"Well, perhaps you could talk about her. I mean, after all, you have a deal with Mr. Ranger to make her feel good about herself. Right?" Herman pulled out a fresh cigar from his inner pocket and promptly lit it with a match.

"I guess. Mr. Ranger did say she was struggling. I suppose I could try and perk her up. I'm ready to just get on with it."

"Ah, I'm sure it won't be all that bad. Be a gentleman, and try your best to entertain her." Herman chuckled mockingly as he inhaled a large puff and devoured the rest of his apple.

"To be honest, I'm growing tired of entertaining women who aren't Opal," I said with a sigh.

"What does that mean?" Herman sat up, eager to dig up the dirt.

"I ran into Dottie a few weeks ago at the post office," I replied, taking a seat on the couch. "She admitted she's had feelings for me.

"She did?" Herman exclaimed, entirely beside himself. "What did you say?"

"I didn't know what to say. Before I knew it, she was leaning in to kiss me," I said, continuing to fidget with my tie.

"And did she?" Herman beamed.

"Of course not!" I replied, slightly annoyed that he would think so. "I told her I didn't feel the same way and that I only wanted her friendship."

"Man, oh, man." Herman shook his head. "Don't get me wrong. I know Opal is definitely the girl for you, but that Dottie is some woman. She says what she wants. She does what she wants. You don't see too many knockouts like her as sure of themselves as she is," Herman declared, continuing to shake his head in disbelief.

"Well, if you feel that way, why don't you court her? A woman like Dottie seems much more your speed anyway," I said sarcastically.

Herman laughed wagging his finger at me and taking another drag from his cigar while a chunk of apple still sat in the pocket of his cheek. "I plan on enjoying a nice night in with the radio and yesterday's paper. No time for women." I rolled my eyes at Herman, sure of myself that he was telling a tale.

"Oh? Is a night with Millie not on the agenda after all? I thought things were going well with the two of you." Herman nodded and gave me a smirk.

"Fine, brother, you caught me. My plans tonight do include Millie. I was merely attempting to keep your thoughts about her as pure as possible since it's already nearing 7:30. I suppose that's the gentleman thing to do. Isn't it?"

An embarrassed expression came across his face, and he attempted to hide it by taking another puff from his cigar. I smiled and nodded at him. "I suppose it is."

I was shocked to hear the words from Herman's lips. He had never been the kind to shy away from discussing a lady in pursuit. It was a strange idea to consider Herman a romancer, private in his love affairs to protect the one he cared for. He has always been a chaser, but I'd never imagined he'd be the one to get caught up in a love affair. I walked into my bedroom, retrieved my coat from the foot of the bed and headed for the door.

"Don't have too much fun tonight, Henry! It'd be a shame if you forgot about your first love." Herman kicked his feet up and waved to me from the couch. I chuckled at him and shook my head.

"Thanks for the advice, Herm. Don't stay out too late." With those last words, I was out the door and on my way to a dinner that I was sure I would not enjoy.

I was a nervous wreck when I arrived at Mr. Ranger's home. He lived in the more developed side of town, only half a mile from the ocean. There was a gentle breeze that followed me inside the front door to the two-story home, as Mrs. Ranger answered promptly after just two knocks. I was greatly surprised to find that she was a very petite woman herself, all done up with a pretty shade of red lipstick applied perfectly on her lips. I had always imagined that she'd be fuller figured since both Cathy and Mr. Ranger were. I could see now that Cathy took solely after her father. "Well, you must be Henry! I'm Mrs. Ranger, but if you'd like, you can call me Betty."

"No, he can't, Bets." Mr. Ranger walked into the foyer to greet me alongside his wife. He pointed his eyebrows up at me and extended his hand to give me a firm shake. "You will call her Mrs. Ranger. Understood?"

"Yes, Sir." I was not about to go against Mr. Ranger. He was a short man but a scary one, nonetheless. I gulped and stood awkwardly in the hall.

"Oh, please, Bobby! Don't you go scarin' him off 'fore Cathy can even get downstairs." Mr. Ranger rolled his eyes at his wife and mouthed out the words again to me when she wasn't looking. *You will call her Mrs. Ranger.*

I cleared my throat and tried to speak assertively. "So, i- is Cathy about ready?"

"Oh, she'll be down shortly. Why don't you make yourself comfortable, Henry? Go sit on the sofa, and I'll pour you some tea." Mrs. Ranger pointed down the hall to their perfectly furnished living room and then disappeared in another direction. Mr. Ranger followed behind me and made himself comfortable in a chair that sat across from the sofa.

"Henry, I'd like to thank you for doing this for my Cathy. I know this all must feel strange given you're involved with someone at the moment."

I felt my face grow a little tight as I sensed myself becoming annoyed with Mr. Ranger. What I wanted to say was, *Well, it isn't like you've given me much of a choice!* But I held my tongue. What I said instead was, "My pleasure, Mr. Ranger. Cathy is a swell girl from what I can remember. It would be an honor to take her out." Mr. Ranger nodded and stretched a proud grin across his face.

"She really is swell. Isn't she?" He leaned back and smiled at the ceiling. I nodded at him and crossed my arms. It was interesting to see the devotion that Mr. Ranger had, all just to make his daughter happy. It made me wonder what kind of father I would be to my own children when the time came with Opal. Would I do anything for them? After getting to know Mr. Ranger, surely in that moment, I believed I would.

"Alright, I've got hot tea coming in, boys." Mrs. Ranger walked in with a tray that held a teapot and three teacups. She placed the tray on the coffee table that sat in the middle of the living room and began to pour. She handed me a cup and smiled brightly at me. Mrs. Ranger really was beautiful. She had a charming maturity to her looks, like a finely aged wine. The crow's feet on the corners of her eyes only seemed to add to her radiance. I smiled back at her as I took a sip from my glass and exhaled deeply from the couch. This was nice. I began to wish it was Opal that I was waiting for and that it was her parents I was getting to know.

"Hello, Henry." A tiny glint of sadness sat in my stomach when Cathy spoke because I knew it wasn't Opal. I turned to see Cathy standing in the archway of the living room all dressed up in a shimmery black cocktail dress that fit her figure nicely. I smiled back politely, relieved to finally be on with this night.

"Cathy, boy, it's good to see you." I stood to greet her. She blushed as I made my way to her, touching her elbow as I leaned in to embrace her. Her makeup was done with extra care, and her reddish-brown hair was curled just right. Mr. Ranger and his wife stood and gazed on us proudly. I began to feel a bit awkward with them staring at us longingly. "Well, Cathy, we uh-better get goin'."

"Yes, of course. Just let me run and fetch my purse." Cathy disappeared up the stairs while I stood and waited with her parents.

"Oh, you two are going to have such a wonderful night! I want to hear all about it when you return," Mrs. Ranger squealed with excitement and kissed my cheek.

"Yes, while we're on the subject of returning, you are to have my Cathy back by no later than nine o'clock. Understood?" Mr. Ranger's cigar breath seeped into my nose as he leaned in and spoke with his chilling tone. It was strange to see Mr. Ranger acting in such a fatherly manner. He was always so harsh and cold on the docks.

"Y-yes, Sir. I'll have Cathy back promptly at nine." I loosened my tie to keep the sweat from settling on my collar. Mr. Ranger grunted and walked down the hall just as Cathy was returning. I linked arms with her. I quickly led her outside, trying to escape any further pressures from her father, my only employer.

We stepped outside into the cool air as the sun began to settle behind a cliff in the distance. The sky darkened as Cathy and I walked along the sidewalk. We were quiet for a time. I couldn't think of anything to say to her. I was used to greeting her in passing on my way into the office when I worked at Edmund's, but this was a different level of acquaintanceship.

"I'm sorry about all this. My daddy can be quite the motivator when he wants to be." Cathy pulled a handkerchief from her purse and dabbed at the tiny beads of sweat that were forming in her palms. I suddenly realized she was just as nervous, if not more so than me.

"That's quite alright. I know he means well. I hope to be just as good a father to my own children someday." We strolled along the sidewalk as the night air began to cool.

"I can tell you will be. You can always tell the good ones from the great ones, and you, Henry, I can tell you're going to make a wonderful father." She smiled coyly to herself and avoided eye contact with me. I felt myself relax a little at her sweet compliment.

"What a nice thing to say. Thank you, Cathy." We crossed the street at the second intersection and headed into town. "So, how are things at the office?"

"Oh, please, Henry. I doubt you wanna hear about the daily bores at Edmund's." Cathy giggled and sifted through her purse, pulling out a fresh stick of chewing gum. She offered it to me, but I politely shook my head no. "All everyone does all day long is type, type, type, until their fingers have gone numb. I got lucky when they pulled me from the floor and decided to make me the office secretary. I just know I would've gone mad after too long." I thought back to my days as a desk clerk. I immediately felt so grateful to have a job as a longshoreman. Being at that desk all day used to feel like self-inflicted torture.

"Yeah, well, I suppose you're right. I never did care much for my position there. I finally get to do something with my hands, and that's a start for me." We approached the restaurant. Luckily for us, most places were within walking distance in San Pedro. *Little Joe's Italian Restaurant* was painted neatly on a sign that stood about twenty feet tall, just outside the restaurant. Mr. Ranger had so graciously called ahead and asked that our bill be placed on his tab, which was a relief for me with my small wages.

"Henry, wait." Cathy grabbed my shoulder and pulled me aside just before we could enter. "I feel I must be honest with you before we go any further."

I nodded at her, trying to be understanding. "What is it, Cathy?" She pulled out the spare gum wrapper from her purse and politely turned away from me to spit out her gum. After a few brief moments of silence, she stood up straight and looked me straight in the eye.

"I'm not fond of you, Henry." I blinked a few times, trying hard not to react to her striking words.

"Excuse me?"

"Well, at least not in that way. Daddy didn't tell me everything, but I know undoubtedly that he forced you on this date tonight." I shook my head at her, trying to refute the words coming out of her mouth. Sadly, I couldn't find any words of my own to do so. "It's alright, Henry. I know you're not the one to blame for this. I just don't want you to feel as if this night means we're courting." I continued to nod but dared not speak even a syllable. "Besides, my father's only doing this to keep me away from Jacob, but it won't do any good."

"Who's Jacob?" I crossed my arms and tapped my chin intrigued to find out where this story would lead.

"I met him a while ago when he was working the cash register at the local grocery store. Daddy didn't approve because of his job. He said Jacob wasn't the kind of man he wanted marrying his little girl."

"Well, why didn't your father get him a job down at the docks? Surely he's got connections; he got me in when there wasn't even room for another hand."

Cathy shook her head in defeat. "He did, for a short time, but Jacob struggled." Cathy wrapped her arms around her waist as if to hide. "You see, he's… like me. Jacob's a larger man, and Daddy had no patience for him. He cut Jacob after just two weeks because he couldn't keep up."

"Has Jacob found work since then?" Tears filled her eyes as she frantically dug through her purse for her handkerchief. She shook her head at me as she lightly dabbed under her eyes.

"No, he went back to the grocery store after Daddy let him go. That was over four years ago. Jacob and I manage to see each other whenever we can, but I know my father will never approve a marriage."

"Gee, Cathy. I had no idea. Your father said you were-"

"Desperate? That I wasn't able to find someone on my own?"

I shrugged my shoulders, suddenly feeling guilty for agreeing to a date that I now realized must have been utterly humiliating for Cathy. "Well, those weren't the words exactly." She nodded and smiled sarcastically as she exchanged her handkerchief for a powder puff.

"Figures. Daddy's been tryin' to sell me off to his version of an ideal husband for years now, but truth be told, I woulda been married a long time ago if he had let me be with Jacob."

"You don't say. Has Jacob already asked for your hand?"

"Five times since we started courting. Each time my father has denied him. He says I can do a lot better than the grocery boy. He says he can find me a better suitor." Tears began to form in her eyes once again, and she swiftly withdrew her handkerchief a second time. After a few moments of silence, she placed all of the items back into her purse and closed it. "I'm sorry. I'm sure you don't want to hear all my grumblings about my personal life. I just wanted to be honest with you."

"No, please don't apologize. I completely understand. Thank you for your honesty." Cathy nodded at me and smiled. "Well, how about we get a bite to eat just as friends. Whaddya say? Would you be up for that?" She smiled at me and nodded. "Aha! There's a smile." Cathy giggled at me and patted my shoulder.

"Oh, Henry. You are so kind," she giggled. I smiled as I led the way toward the restaurant doors. "I'm sure you'll make a fine husband to Dottie someday, when the time is right, of course." My stomach twisted into a thousand knots, hearing Cathy's words. Hell, did the whole town think Dottie and I were an item? I ignored Cathy's remark in an attempt to ease myself from the discomfort, despite my inner urge to run for the hills. I opened the door to the restaurant and motioned for Cathy to step inside.

"Shall we?"

Chapter Nine

Opal

San Pedro CA
March 21, 1929

Sweetheart,

I have not heard from you for so long. It seems months and months, but I guess it has not been so long. I sure have missed your sweet letters the last few days and hope that I have one before this reaches you. How are you by now, dear one? I hope you are well. I know you are just as lovely as ever and more so to me now that I can feel so sure of you really being mine one of these sweet days. Dearest babe, our future looks better every day, and how I do hope that it will really materialize into something very profitable for us. Of course, the climax has not been reached as yet, but, dearest, win or lose, I'll carry on with your love. And as my finances begin to provide, I hope that before many months have passed, I can receive my world's best and life's sweetest reward. And you babe, are the one big prize I am counting. Sweetheart, I can think of so much more, but as for now, we'll chase and go to bed. This is now 12:30 am, so goodbye and goodnight, dear.

Henry

Guilt set in as I read over the words two more times. I wasn't avoiding Henry; I was simply trying to honor Thomas' wishes to consider his proposal. I laid in my bed, even though it was almost noon, and grazed my fingers over the words that Henry wrote. I wanted nothing more than to be with him, but I also knew that Thomas made a good point. I had my entire family to look after.

In that moment, I wished I could go back to the old times when Henry was still in St. Louis, and our relationship made sense to everyone. Life was so simple then. It made me giggle to myself to remember Henry and his bold character. He didn't waste any time coming to find me the day after he was thrown out of the soldier's ball. I could almost picture it clearly in my head, moment for moment.

I had woken up bright and early on account of having to work at the print shop that morning. I kept finding myself daydreaming about the night before. Henry was so breathtaking. The very thought of him brought a chill to my shoulders. I stepped outside two hours after I had arrived for work to run and fetch the mail for Mrs. Colt, my superior. Mrs. Colt was a mean old lady who seemed to take pleasure in seeing her employees suffer. I was lucky enough to get a break from her twice a week when she would send me on errands to fetch things for the shop. That's when I ran into Henry.

I had barely made it off the curb just outside the shop when he walked right behind me and covered my eyes with his palms. "Guess who?" I tried to answer, but before I'd even had a chance to get a word out, Henry appeared in front of me dressed as dapper as ever.

"Henry! How on earth did you find me?" I gasped as I threw my arms around him, beaming with excitement. He chuckled to himself and withdrew a crumpled rose from his inner jacket pocket.

"Mr. Penny, from the shoe store. He told me you worked just a block over from him. I hope you don't mind. I had to come see you." His bashful expression was so endearing. I found myself not able to concentrate. He handed me the crumpled rose, brought my hand up to his mouth and pecked it gently. "It's a little rough around the edges but still the most beautiful flower."

I smiled and accepted his gift without delay. "Thank you. I think it's perfect."

"I think you're perfect." His eyes became so focused when he said this; his stares were so intentional. It was as if he didn't want to miss a beat. I felt myself blush, but I couldn't resist bringing my eyes back to his. After a few silent moments, I finally came back to where I was, standing on the sidewalk in the middle of downtown.

"Well… I'd better be on my way." He reached for my shoulder in hopes to detain me, as if doing so would also delay the moment.

"Oh, do ya have to go so soon? I was hopin' we could spend some time together." I suddenly felt very overwhelmed. I had only met this man a few days ago, and already I was feeling so attached to him. Every emotion from excitement to terror came creeping in on me at once. I gently pulled away from his touch and straightened my coat.

"I'm sorry. I have errands to run for the print shop. Mrs. Colt is very strict about punctuality. Perhaps some other time." I started to walk toward downtown, but Henry was eager.

"Well, perhaps I could meet your folks some time? If it's alright with you, I'd very much so like to court you. When can I meet your father?" A twinge of anger boiled inside me as he uttered the words. How dare he mention my father so insensitively without even pausing to consider that perhaps I no longer had one! I turned back to face him with a cold expression and practically yelled back my response without even flinching.

"My father died a long time ago. How crass can you be?" The look on Henry's face said it all. He was completely mortified. I didn't try at all to ease his conscience. I was suddenly annoyed with him. "Perhaps you should have spent a little more time digging into my history before approaching me next." I threw the rose back at him and turned around, treading down the sidewalk and stamping my feet as loudly as I could as I stormed off. I could hear Henry calling to me, but I was so mad. I couldn't even bother to turn back. There was one thing I knew I would never tolerate, and that was people disrespecting my papa.

I didn't see Henry for a whole two weeks following that incident. I was sure he had gotten the message. I really couldn't have cared less during that hiatus. I figured I had scared him off, and for good reason. I remember it had been two weeks exactly, two Mondays after I had seen Henry outside the print shop. I had just returned from running an errand for Mrs. Colt. She was in no mood for nonsense.

"Opal? Is that you walking in?" she crowed from the back room.

"Yes, Mrs. Colt. Just returning from the supply store."

"You're late," she said strictly. I rolled my eyes at her annoying remarks and set the paper bag full of items she had commissioned me to get on the counter.

"Yes, ma'am. I apologize for the delay, but the supply store didn't have the right magnifying glass you were looking for. I had to run across town to another shop just to find it." Mrs. Colt stomped into the front with her hands on her hips just to look at me with anger.

"What have I told you about excuses, girl?" I sighed and smoothed out my skirt.

"They can't right your mistakes." She nodded at me in approval and walked towards the counter to ensure the items I had purchased for her were correct. She pulled an envelope from her apron and handed it to me while she rustled through her goods. "This came for you while you were out. The poor fellow didn't want to give it to you in person. You must've scared him off with all your excuses." Mrs. Colt chuckled to herself, proud of her simple joke.

I took the envelope from her and read the face. All it said was my name in large letters. I quickly tore it open and stepped away to a corner by the window to read it. It read:

Opal,

I am writing this letter to you because I was not sure if you'd ever want to see me again after the way I acted before. I am truly sorry for my insensitivity. I should have asked about your parents before assuming something so incredibly unsympathetic. And I want you to know that I am deeply sorrowful about the loss of your father, truly I am. I'm sure I can't even imagine such pain.

And so, in his honor and yours, I looked up your father, and I went to visit his stone. I laid a rose on his grave as a way to undo my wrongs and personally apologize to him for hurting his daughter. I hope that is alright with you.

I understand if you have no interest in my courtship, but perhaps we can continue a friendship. Take all the time you need, dear Opal.

Truly,

Henry

My tears felt like tiny needles prying their way out of my eyes. I tried to conceal my sobs, but it was to no avail. I quickly wrapped the letter inside its envelope and reached for my coat.

"Good heavens, child, what is the matter with you?" Mrs. Colt said, seeming both concerned and annoyed with me. I tried to speak through my cries but could not successfully produce anything audible. I quickly swung my coat over my shoulders and ran out of the shop. In fact, I kept running. I ran all the way there. I needed to see it. I needed to see if he had really done it.

The cemetery was only a few blocks out of town. I ran through the pain of sore ankles from doing errands for Mrs. Colt all afternoon.

I arrived at the cemetery after running for almost fifteen minutes. I quickly ran past the entrance. It had two large iron gates that remained open until five o'clock. I paced through the rows of headstones until I found his. I brought my hand to my mouth when I realized he was telling the truth. Sitting in the middle of my papa's headstone was the crumpled rose I had thrown at Henry two weeks ago. Tied to it by a piece of twine was a new rose, just barely in full blossom.

I fell to my knees at the sight and clutched my chest. It was this moment that separated Henry from all the rest. That was the first letter I had ever received from Henry. After that day, I knew it was going to be him.

Chapter Ten

Henry

"You workin' the crane today, Herman?" I was practically yelling over all of the commotion on the dock that Friday morning. Fridays were often our most stressful days because Mr. Ranger liked us to double-check the entire inventory on week's end. Herman nodded and gave me a thumbs-up as he started a light jog towards the west port.

"Yep! I'll see you later, Henry. I wanna hear all about your date with Cathy during lunch." He let out an obnoxious howl and winked at me as he found his way to the other side of the port. I shook my head at him and watched him grow smaller in the distance before I headed to my own station.

I was placed on rigging duty. There were three workers assigned to a unit for every container we loaded: Chip Dunham, a rather muscular man who stood about six-foot-five and Ives Autry, a Frenchman who barely spoke English. Both were part of my unit. By the time I got to my station, Harvey was already rigging up a load, and Ives was diligently documenting information on a clipboard.

“Morning fellas,” I spoke candidly, my mind was still wrapped up in the previous night. Cathy and I had a nice time once she opened up about her relationship with Jacob, the grocery boy. It gave me a chance to open up to her about Opal. I told her all about the awkward dealings with Dottie that had taken place over the past few weeks and how Dottie had admitted to having feelings for me.

I was expecting Cathy to relate to Dottie, seeing as how she knows her and has worked with her for some time. To my surprise, Cathy completely understood my side. She even gave me some plain advice on how to break the stiffness between Dottie’s and my friendship. It felt good to make a friend in Cathy that night. It was exactly the encouragement I needed to stay driven in my pursuit of Opal.

“Mornin,’ Champ! ‘Bout time you graced us with your presence.” Harvey was a jokester, always trying to turn the simplest of things into humor.

“Ah, it is a good morning, Henry.” Ives’ accent was still very strong, but I could tell he was trying hard to mask it.

“How many loads you done so far?” I said, scratching my head underneath my cap and shielding my eyes from the sun to look up at Harvey. He was standing on top of one of the cargo containers and pulling tight on a connecting rope.

“Just two so far. Ranger’s got us picking up the slack from the west port today. Plus, we got in a shipment that wasn’t scheduled to come ‘til next week. We’re gonna be behind all day,” Harvey declared. He jumped down from the container and stuck his landing so well you could have easily mistaken him for an Olympic gymnast. “Hey, you hear about Wilbur?” he said, eyes suddenly wide open. I shook my head at Harvey as he dusted his hands off on his pants. I didn’t know Wilbur. I barely talked to the men at the other ports, too many names to remember. “Got his foot sliced pretty bad doin’ a rigging this morning. It was gruesome. Blood was everywhere. They had to stick a towel in his mouth to keep him from hollerin’.”

“How in the hell did he do that?” I said, trying to keep my breakfast down as my stomach churned. Harvey shook his head at me.

"Don't know. Not minding the rope, I guess." Harvey adjusted his pants and continued to shake his head.

"He was not thinking. He connected rigging to the wrong side of cargo." Ives didn't even bother to look up from his clipboard as he spoke.

"You know what the worst thing is? Management ain't even gon' give him the time off to heal. They say his injury is not their responsibility. Poor ol' Wilbur's gonna have to look for work again once his foot heals."

"My God, can they really do that?" I asked, absolutely shocked. Harvey nodded. I knew Mr. Ranger could be a tough man, but I didn't think he'd go so far as to fire a man who'd been injured on the job.

"It ain't about if they can. They did. That's all that matters now. That's what happens when you ain't got a union to back you up. Same thing happened to my cousin 'bout a year ago." Harvey walked up the dock, shaking his head all the while. Ives followed quickly behind him with the clipboard, ready to receive our next container.

I thought about Harvey's words. Were our jobs really on the line all the time? The thought brought an uneasy feeling to my core, and I quickly tried to ignore it. Thinking positively was my only resource. Saving enough money to send for Opal was not up for debate. I was going to do it, even if I had to work my fingers to the bone to get her here.

It wasn't long before the three of us were well into our work. We worked through our scheduled break time and ended up stopping at three-thirty for lunch. Management didn't provide us with a place to eat our lunch, so most of the time all the workers just found a place far enough away from the dock to get away from the noise.

Herman and I didn't eat together that day due to my late break time. I wound up sitting with my unit on the dirt while we cracked open our homemade lunches and inhaled the seemingly *not-enough* sandwiches. I only got halfway through mine before a young fellow came walking toward the three of us as we sat and relaxed. He was a thin fellow, and he couldn't have been any older than sixteen.

"Pardon, Sir. Your name Henry?" I nodded back at the kid and took another bite. "Ranger wants to see you." He walked away before I could answer him. I could feel my heart begin to pound a little faster.

"Damn, you only been here three weeks, and already you got the boss callin' on you for favors?" Harvey joked, but I sensed a hint of jealousy in his tone. I wished I could have assured him that he did not want to be in my shoes, but I knew better than to break the confidentiality of Mr. Ranger.

I stood up and collected the rest of my lunch. "Gentlemen, I guess I'll see you on the docks."

"Yeah, I guess so." Harvey pulled out a pipe and took a match to its bowl. Ives didn't bother responding. He was too involved in his lunch to care.

I headed for the docks and thought of what I would tell Mr. Ranger about my previous night with Cathy. My mind wandered in a million directions. I knew I had to keep my head on straight if I was going to survive working for Robert Ranger.

"Henry, why don't you have a seat?" Ranger pointed to the chair that sat on the other side of his desk. "Close the door, will ya?"

"Yes, Sir." I nodded and shut the door tightly behind me and quickly made my way over to the empty seat.

"I assume you know why I've called you in." Mr. Ranger raised his eyebrows at me and folded his hands over his large belly as he leaned back in his chair.

"I suppose I do. To talk about Cathy? Y-you wanna know how my night went with Cathy, Sir?"

"Oh, no, no, no, no." He wagged his finger at me and laughed angrily. "I know how your night went with Cathy." I shifted in my chair, already uncomfortable with Mr. Ranger's tone. "Cathy told me the two of you had a great night. In fact, it went so well that you encouraged her to stand up to me about some grocery boy named Jacob!" He continued to laugh angrily.

"No, Sir! I would never do that." I could feel the panic setting into my lungs as I tried to exhale an excuse. "I merely told her that if Jacob could meet your requirements, then he would be her best suitor since they already have a relationship."

"Dammit, Henry! That was not a part of the deal!" Mr. Ranger's face grew red as he sat forward and pointed his finger at me. "Your job was to take her out and convince her that she could have anyone else!"

"Pardon me, Sir. But you weren't exactly innocent in this arrangement either."

"And how is that, son?"

"Cathy told me that you've been sending her off on all sorts of dates, trying to wed her to your ideal fellow. You told me this wasn't a romantic engagement. I was to take Cathy out to encourage her, not get her to fall in love with me!"

"How dumb can you be? You think I would have sent you out with her if I weren't hoping it would go somewhere?" A tiny spray of spit came out of his mouth. He pulled out a handkerchief and dabbed at the corners of his mouth.

My eyes widened, and I realized that Mr. Ranger was never going to free me from my obligations to him. I was going to be stuck under his thumb as long as he was my superior. Mr. Ranger covered his eyes with his right hand.

"My Cathy isn't gonna settle down with some boy who works at the market just so they can struggle for the rest of their lives." He waved his free hand at me in an attempt to shoo me away. "Outta my sight, Viefhaus. I'll figure out what I'm gonna do with you on Monday."

"Sir, you can't possibly expect me to knowingly entertain your daughter when I'm currently courting another woman." I tried to humble my tone in an attempt to reason with him.

"I said outta my sight, Viefhaus! See me first thing Monday morning." I nodded and took my leave before he could make any hasty decisions.

"Yes, Sir."

I worked the rest of the day in silence. I wanted to be angry, but I knew I couldn't afford to be. This was the best job I'd had since I took the leap of faith to come to California. The money was good, and the hours were consistent. The worst part about it was management, and I guess most of us workers supposed it was an even trade.

I thought about the Wilbur fellow who'd sliced open his foot and, in turn, had to forfeit his job altogether. I didn't want to end up like him. I couldn't.

The next morning, I woke up early and headed straight to the local library. A sweet old woman sat at the front desk. She had tiny glasses that sat at the tip of her nose, and she was reading the current events section of the newspaper. I instantly thought of Milford from the post office and how perfect a couple Milford and the librarian would make. They had so many similarities; they were practically male and female versions of each other.

"Hello, I'm Margaret, the librarian. Welcome to the *San Pedro Library*," she spoke sweetly. A few strands from her grey hair brushed over her eyebrows, and she quickly tucked them behind her ear.

"Hello, Margaret. I'm Henry."

"What can I do for you today, Henry?" Her smile was warm and inviting.

"I was wondering if you might have any books on union workers?" Margaret nodded at me and stood behind the desk. To my surprise, she was even smaller than I assumed. She might've been the tiniest woman I had ever seen.

"As a matter of fact, we do. Right this way, dear." I followed behind Margaret as she led me up and down aisles of books until we reached a small corner in the back of the library. "Here we are. We have a total of twenty-three books on union working at the moment. Let me know if you need any help."

Margaret hobbled away. She made her way back to the front of the library, leaving me to dive into the endless copies of books and commentaries. I suddenly felt overwhelmed. But I knew I didn't have the luxury of becoming flustered, not if I was going to win my job security.

A flash of Opal ran through my mind. Her beauty was so radiant and luminescent to me now. I could almost envision her standing right in front of me.

"Everything I do is for you, babe," I whispered.

Chapter Eleven

Opal

"Opal, Mama says come downstairs and iron your dress for tonight." Nettie poked her head into my room with mahogany curls that bounced above her shoulders. I turned from my vanity to see her eyes barely peeking in from behind the doorframe.

"I'll be right down." I sighed in the mirror and finished pinning my hair. Thomas and the Reverend Stone were generously taking my entire family to dinner tonight, so we could get better acquainted with my assumed husband to be. The whole thing was Mama's idea. After she'd heard about my slip-up at lunch the other day with calling Thomas by Henry's name, she felt it was time Thomas and I finalized the status of our relationship.

"I won't have you waste another minute in that fantasy head of yours," she'd said, as a way to keep me from arguing. "You'll accept Thomas' proposal, and we'll have the wedding as soon as possible."

I never listened to her. I knew it was all just her way of saying she was worried about me getting older and wanting me to settle down with someone, a wealthy someone. I picked up the brush sitting on the vanity and began to brush my hair as my reflection stared blankly back at me.

I imagined a life with Thomas. I could so clearly picture it. Thomas and I enjoying a hot cup of tea on the front porch of our large house, a property that would sit on no less than three acres of land in the countryside, away from all the noise of downtown. Thomas' practice would be even more extensive than it already is now. Our home would become a place for corporate events and political parties. The mayor would be a frequent dinner guest of ours on account of my cooking skills and Thomas' sizable donation to the city treasury once a year. With so many rooms, we could fit Mama, the twins and their spouses, and all the children they could have. Still, we'd have room for extended family to visit us on holiday.

I imagined myself being the perfect wife, dripping with pearls and diamonds, up to speed with the current fashions and trends. We would have plenty of children, all hand-delivered by Thomas himself - he would say that he didn't trust anyone but himself to deliver our precious babies. Thomas would even care for Mama in her old age. When his medicine wasn't enough, he'd pay for the finest doctors to visit us and tend to Mama's aid.

The life seemed so real, as if it were a prophecy of my coming future. However, seeing myself with Thomas, even in my imagination, saddened me.

"Opal Pleasant, I won't call for you again!" Mama hollered from downstairs. I hopped up from my stool at the vanity and made my way to the kitchen.

"Yes, Ma'am!"

Once downstairs, I skipped into the kitchen just as Mama was removing a pin from her beautiful dark brown hair. The most beautiful curl fell to her face, and she quickly twisted it to the side of her head and replaced the pin. She was only wearing her slip, but her face was done up so beautifully. I couldn't resist admiring her from the doorway. She quickly caught my eye and waved for me to come into the kitchen.

"Well, don't just stand there, girl. Get on with your ironing. The Reverend will be here soon." She seemed anxious, but she always was before company arrived at the house. She wouldn't allow a single thing to be out of place.

"Mama, you look so elegant!" I drifted into her presence, letting the scent of her perfume carry me in. Mama rolled her eyes and gave an accidental smirk that I was sure she was trying to hide.

"Don't be so dramatic, Opal. We're going to dinner. Am I supposed to wear my kitchen clothes and apron?" I shook my head no but continued to beam at her radiance. Her green eyes seemed to sparkle perfectly in the orange and yellow hues from the onset of the evening.

"I hope to look just like you someday, Mama." This time Mama gave me a genuine look, baring her seemingly flawless smile.

"Oh, dear. You always were the doting type, my child." She tilted my chin up to her and pecked my forehead. "I suppose I can admire that, sweet girl." She slipped out of the kitchen, leaving only the aroma of her womanly scent behind. I smiled to myself as I placed my dress across the flat sheet that Mama had lain over the kitchen table. I was proud to be her daughter. We may not have had the fanciest clothes, but no one could deny that the Pleasant women had unmistakable beauty.

Dinner with Thomas and Reverend Stone was tranquil and then, all at once, very noisy. Thomas took us all to *Al's Restaurant*. It was one of St. Louis' up and coming restaurants known for serving some of the best steak around. I knew he chose it to impress Mama and the Reverend, but I wasn't complaining. At this point, I had decided to let Mama and Thomas do as they pleased. Truth be told, I didn't care where we ate. I was too nervous thinking about my final answer to Thomas that I could have been served mud soup and not known the difference.

Mama, Reverend Stone and Thomas kept up most of the conversation while I merely chimed in every so often with a word or two when Mama would give me the eye. The twins didn't talk to the adults at all. They were much too wrapped up in their secret language to be bothered with the table talk.

"That's when he did it. He handed me a small needle and thread and said, 'what are you gonna do now, Tommy?' So, I'm shaking in my boots as my pa and my brother are just starin' at me. At this point, the wolf has run off, and poor Minnie's got wounds so bad. It was almost too gruesome to look at. Then, without another moment's thought, I picked up my hound, who at this point is bleeding profusely, and I whisper to her, 'You're gonna be alright, Minnie.' It felt like only a few seconds, but I know it had to be minutes before I had her stitched up and carried to the car. She died on our way to the veterinarian's office. That was when I knew I wanted to practice medicine, just like my pa. I needed to prove to myself that I was good enough to save a life," Thomas said, finishing his dramatic story. Mama clutched her pearls, wholly moved by Thomas' words. I rolled my eyes at all the attention he was getting.

"Oh, Thomas, what a moving story," Mama said with a subtle sigh. "How old did you say you were again?" Mama dabbed away a tear that had welled in her left eye.

"Fourteen. My younger brother Clay was only ten at the time. I knew he'd be devastated if we didn't at least try to save Minnie." Mama shook her head in disbelief at Thomas.

"Truly a remarkable tale, Thomas." Reverend Stone took a sip from his water glass and dragged his finger around the rim. "You ever go fishin' anymore after that incident?"

Thomas shook his head no at the Reverend.

"Unfortunately not. While the story yielded a positive outcome, the memory of losing Minnie is still too painful to go back." Everyone nodded their heads in unison at Thomas, utterly sympathetic to his emotional trauma.

"Well, Thomas, Opal, I'd like to propose a toast to your new engagement." My eyes widened at the Reverend's careless use of the word engagement, despite my not having officially declared a yes. Mama raised her glass of wine simultaneously with the Reverend's glass. She gazed at the two of us with pride in her eyes and intuition on her lips as she formed a knowing smile. Thomas and I shared a look. His expression alluded that he knew I had neither confirmed nor denied the proposal but that also he wouldn't mind if I gave him an answer immediately. Thomas raised his glass to the Reverend, nodding at me to gesture that we should respectfully play along.

“May the two of you be prosperous and ever-faithful as our Lord Father in Heaven,” the Reverend said with a sparkle in his eye. A moment of silence fell for a brief moment, and then all at once, we were clinking glasses and smiling, thanking the Reverend for his kind words and well wishes. Once the table had calmed, Thomas finally cut in.

“Thank you, Reverend Stone, for those precious remarks. It truly is an honor to have your blessing.” Thomas shot me a quick side-eye as he squirmed in his chair, too anxious to go on. “However, Opal and I have not finalized the status of our… relationship just yet.”

The Reverend frowned, obviously displeased. Mama cut me a look that said I was to blame for this awkward breach in our night. “I see. Well, you’ve been courting long enough. What’s it been, about five-six months now? Opal, dear, hasn’t he proposed? I was sure I was told that Thomas had asked for your hand. Was I not?”

I nodded my head quickly to appease the Reverend’s inquiries, but I could not find the words to respond to his disappointments.

“Uh- Opal just hasn’t found it in her heart yet to say yes, Reverend.” Thomas cut in, and I was so relieved that he had. “She’s a brilliant girl. She knows marriage is a great commitment - one that shouldn’t be taken lightly. Respectfully, she wants to be sure that she is considering all that it means to give her all to someone, Reverend.”

The Reverend’s eyes slowly drifted from Thomas to me. He tapped his fingers on the edge of the table, searching my face for answers. “Well, perhaps Opal is ready to give you an answer now.” Reverend Stone’s eyes didn’t move an inch from mine as he challenged me. My eyes widened, and Mama beamed.

“I agree, Reverend Stone. I think the two of them have had more than enough time to consider it.” Mama took another sip from her wine. I couldn’t tell if her bold response was out of sheer annoyance from how long I was taking to give Thomas an answer or if the ‘Jesus Juice’ had taken over her coherent ability. The Reverend nodded at Mama with a tight grin, likely angered after making a fool of himself just moments before.

"Well, Opal. I'm sure by now you've made up your mind on the subject. No sense in making the poor fellow wait any longer, how agonizing!"

"With all due respect, Reverend Stone, I think this is a subject that Opal and I should discuss in private." Thomas reached for my hand on the table and squeezed gently.

"Nonsense. If it's an answer for you, then it's an answer for all of us. Now Opal, give Thomas an answer, so we can be done with this foolishness."

Thomas glanced at me and gave me an *I tried* expression. He nodded, supportive of the oncoming truth. Here it was. After all these weeks of putting it off, I no longer had any more time to myself to think.

"I-I," was all I could manage to stammer out. Thomas squeezed my hand once more.

"It's alright, Opal. You can tell me the truth," Thomas said. He gave me a forced smile. Behind those eyes, I could tell he was just as scared to hear the truth as I was to tell it. I gave a final sigh as I locked eyes with Thomas, afraid of how he would react once I had answered.

"Oh, get on with it, child! I will not tolerate this any longer." Mama was emboldened by her Cabernet and the Reverend's validation. She was by no means drunk, but she was feeling more inclined to divulge her private opinions. She pointed a finger at me and pursed her lips. "Opal Pleasant, you tell this man *yes* right now!"

I inhaled a subtle breath and looked at Thomas, his eyes hopeful but already full of disappointment. He turned toward me and feigned a smile as he brought my hand into his chest.

"So, what'll it be, Opal?" he said. I smiled politely back at him. All eyes were on me now; even the twins were deeply engaged at this point. I had almost forgotten the twins were party to this whole event. I nodded back at him.

"Yes, Thomas. I will marry you."

Chapter Twelve

Henry

I waited in the seating area of the management office for 45 minutes before Mr. Ranger finally called me in. I was there first thing Monday, just as he'd demanded, anticipating my imminent release.

"Mr. Viefhaus, are you alright?" I came out of my daze of counting the checkered tiles on the floor to find Mrs. Waller, Mr. Ranger's secretary, standing in front of me with her arms folded and a look of concern riddled across her face. She had her light brown hair pinned back in a neat bun with a pencil coming out the top of it.

"Fine, thanks," I lied. She nodded unbelievingly.

"Alright. Well, Mr. Ranger is ready to see you now." I stood to my feet and inhaled all the air I could.

Mr. Ranger was in no mood to pretend this morning, all business as soon as I entered his office.

"Shut the door, Liz," he said rudely.

Mrs. Waller wasted no time closing the door tightly behind me. I stood with my arms folded behind me like I was a schoolteacher conducting a lesson.

"Henry, sit."

"Yes, Sir." I obeyed. Mr. Ranger stared at me a long while, torturing me before he finally decided to open his mouth and put me out of my misery.

"Henry," Mr. Ranger said flatly as he rolled his next words around in his head, "I've decided I'm not gonna fire you."

"Oh, thank you, Sir." I sat back, relieved. I realized just then that I had been holding my breath the whole time. Mr. Ranger put a hand up to shush me.

"Don't get too happy just yet, my boy." Mr. Ranger folded his hands over his belly and sat back. "I want you to take Cathy out again."

"Sir, you can't be serious!" I reacted almost simultaneously to his words. I was so anxious. I was certain my heart had fallen through the bottom of my seat. "I cannot continue to see your daughter while courting another woman. You must see the conflict in that - don't you?"

"For God's sake, Viefhaus, contain yourself, and let me finish!" Mr. Ranger huffed and reached into his top drawer, revealing a fresh cigar. He cut the end of it and took a match to its tip and gave a few small puffs to get it started. "Now listen here." He used his cigar as a pointer. "I'm tired of fighting Cathy on the matter of this, Jacob fellow. It's clear she's never going to listen to me on the subject, so I've decided to consider this Jacob once again."

"I think that's great, Sir!" I manage to say without adding a sigh of relief. "Then, may I ask why you need me to take Cathy out again?"

"I just want to be certain," he said after a brief pause to consider the question, shaking a hopeless fist in the air. "I want to be sure that there's no way she might fall for another. I want to see if maybe she'll realize she's wrong about that pudgy fellow and marry someone decent."

I eyed Mr. Ranger's belly for a brief moment in awe that he could even utter such words. "With all due respect, Mr. Ranger," I said calmly, trying my best to tread lightly. "Cathy told me she's loved Jacob for four years without any promises of marriage. I think if she were gonna give up, she'd have done so by now."

Mr. Ranger sat back up with a look of grief written across his face as he pondered what I'd said. I could almost see the cogs turning in his head as he searched for another solution.

"I can't accept that," he said solemnly while shaking his head. "She's just confused. I mean, how's a woman to know what's best for her?"

"Sir," I said, daring to interrupt. "With all due respect, Cathy's a woman, not a child. Consider your wife for thought. How long did it take before she knew that you were right for her? A year? Two years? I'll bet your courtship never came close to four years."

I sat in my chair and waited for Mr. Ranger to tear me a new one for daring to speak on his marriage. His eyes remained fixated on mine for what seemed to be long, dragging hours. His face was stern, and I couldn't tell if he was consumed with rage or allowing my words to settle.

"I suppose you're right," he finally sighed, allowing his defeat to settle in. Mr. Ranger leaned back in his chair and took another drag from his cigar. He looked at me and nodded, tapping the butt of his cigar in an ashtray at the corner of his desk without looking.

"What is it about that kid?" Though Mr. Ranger asked the question out loud, I knew I didn't need to answer it. "He's got his hooks so deep into my Cathy. I'm not sure she'll ever see clearly."

"I suppose it's love, Sir," I proposed, watching the disappointment set in on his shoulders. Mr. Ranger nodded in bitter agreement.

"You're a good kid, Viefhaus," he admitted. "What do you say we forget about all this nonsense, huh? You can go back to just being the new kid who stays out of trouble."

"I'd like that very much, Mr. Ranger," I said, nodding thankfully.

"Attaboy," Mr. Ranger said, still sounding defeated. "Now, out of my sight. Get some dock beneath your shoes."

"Yes, Sir." I smiled and stood from my chair. I promptly shook his hand, escaping his office as quickly as my feet would take me.

My workday seemed to flash before my eyes. Before I knew it, the time had struck 4 o'clock, and Herman and I were heading towards the bus stop. I told Herman I'd meet him at home after I ran a few errands.

My first stop was the *San Pedro Library*. I decided I would go every day after work to study union formation and the process of getting one organized. That day I was pleased to read an article from a New York paper that was dated back to 1912. The author, Sean Stanton, had dedicated an entire page to discussing the matter and was remarkably thorough in his research. He surprisingly was able to predict strikes and rebellions that, at the time, he could not have known anything about. He stated that if the East Coast docks didn't shape up and pay their workers a decent wage or protect their rights, there were bound to be uprisings, as well as an increase in workers sitting out in demonstrative protest. He even went on to discuss the economy of New York and other east-coast states. Stanton stated that the organization of a union would only prove to benefit each state's economic pull, thus strengthening the purchasing power of the workers to drive the economy upward.
I speedily took notes on everything I read. By the time I looked back on all I had written, my poor notes looked more like chicken scratches than words.

"I'm sorry to bother you, dear. But the library is closing now. You'll have to come back tomorrow." I looked up to find Margaret, the librarian, smiling sweetly at me. "Would you like me to set these items aside for you?"

"Yes, please." I nodded and stood from my desk in the back corner of the library. I gathered my papers and patted the tiny old woman on the shoulder.

"I'll be back tomorrow, Margaret. Thank you."

I withdrew my watch from my right pocket to find it was already 6:02 pm. It felt like I had only been in the library for a few minutes. I wondered to myself how I could let so much time slip away.

The evening air felt crisp against my face as I made the trek home. I passed by a couple on the sidewalk holding hands and laughing to themselves. It was then that I realized I hadn't once thought about Opal. I was so caught up in the stress of meeting with Mr. Ranger and then studying at the library that I never got a chance to think about anything else.

I crossed the street and found myself entering the post office without a moment's thought. Milford's eyes widened, and a smile slid up his cheeks when he saw me.

"Henry! How are ya, my boy?" he exclaimed, taking a puff from the pipe dangling from his bottom lip.

"Fine, Milford." I smiled and extended my hand to his over the counter. "Say, have you got any letters for me back there?"

"Hmm, let me check on that for ya," Milford said as he tapped his chin and disappeared into the back. Moments later, he reappeared empty-handed and gave me a light sigh. "Sorry, Henry, nothing in today. You expecting somethin'?"

"No, not exactly," I said, disappointed.

I tried to remember the last letter I received from Opal, but I couldn't seem to recall it. An immediate feeling that something must be wrong washed over me as I remembered the last letter I sent, questioning why she hadn't written in a while. The insecurity that Opal might be done with me caused a numbness unfamiliar to me.

"Could I borrow some paper, Milford, and a pen if you have it?"

"Sure thing, Henry!" Milford handed me a pen and retrieved two sheets of blank paper from behind the counter. "Take all the time you need. I'll be right back." Milford puffed at his pipe some more and disappeared into the back of the store.

I tried to think of the right words to say to Opal. I didn't know what was happening, but I knew I felt uneasy.

San Pedro, CA
April 9, 1929

Opal dear,

I am only writing a few lines tonight, babe, to remind you again of your man and his love for you. I am still here, awaiting even just a few lines from you. It feels so long since last I've heard from you. Your silence makes me fear something terrible has happened. Please write to me and tell me that my darling girl is alright.

Honey, dear, I'm just so lonely, so blue. For dear one, I'm so far away from you - from the girl of my dreams. You are my life and my desire. Oh baby doll, you can't realize how I love you, how essential you are to me and my future life, sweetheart. I pray it won't be so long until you are in my arms. For if I can't come to you soon, I'm going to send you expenses. And I want you to meet me here. If I go broke and have to work, I hope that you will consider all the trouble you may have to experience in married life with a poor boy for a mate.

Whereas, if I can only be fortunate to find success, I will be able to do what I have wanted to for two years - to give you a home, happiness, health and love. Rest assured, my darling love, you will have in abundance. For you are my one, little dream-girl. I'm praying it won't be long until you are mine. But I find consolation in the fact that someday soon, you can be called "my own" and I, "your own." Think of that, so sweet, that is as I write it. "Our own." Opal dear, I will wait patiently for your next letter. I should hope it won't be long.

Affectionately yours,

Henry

I folded the letter and stuffed it in an empty envelope that Milford had left on the counter for me. The old man still wasn't back yet, so I wrote the address on the face of the envelope and sealed the letter. After placing it in the outgoing box, I slipped out quietly before he could return.

The fresh air, once again, washed over my face as I was reintroduced to the night air. I walked a long way, observing people on the streets before I realized I was supposed to stop by the market to pick up more potatoes. Herman loved potatoes and always ate them all before I could get to them. Luckily, the market was just a block away.

Braverman Market was the only market in town that closed at seven o'clock. They were independently owned, and I assumed the owners could do without the late hours for little profit. If you wanted a market open later than that, you'd have to travel out of town for it.

I had the store memorized like the back of my hand. Once inside, I quickly found the produce aisle and picked out five beautifully ripened potatoes. I cradled the spuds to my chest as if my produce were an infant. I headed back down my aisle towards the cash register but stopped in my tracks when I heard a familiar laugh, a woman's laugh, coming from the aisle next to mine.

"Oh, stop it! You are not a chef!" The woman's voice giggled.

"Oh, yeah? Then how is it that you liked the pork I made for you last week?" a man's voice answered, another familiar voice.

"Oh, please, Jeffrey. You can't pull the wool over my eyes. You told me your sister always gives you half of everything she cooks on account of your bachelor lifestyle." The woman giggled. My eyes closed as I pieced together the inevitable.

"Well, sure, but I heated it back up for you, didn't I?" I looked up to the heavens and asked God why he was humoring himself at my expense.

I followed the voices to the end of my aisle, trying ever so carefully to confirm with a quick look down the other side without being noticed. My suspicions were put to rest as I undoubtedly saw Jeffrey, my former boss, with his arm around none other than Dottie herself. The pair continued to laugh as I tried to sneak away towards the cash register unnoticed, but I was too late.

"Henry!" Dottie's voice cracked as I could hear the panic in her voice. She quickly shoved her way out of Jeffrey's arms as if I was her father and had caught her with a boy I had previously forbidden. Jeffrey's hurt expression said it all as he turned his eyes from Dottie to mine with a look of anger dancing in his eyes. I knew what he was thinking because I had the exact dialogue with God in my head too. What the hell was I doing here?

"Y-you shop at the *Braverman Market*?" Dottie asked, trying to hide her nerves.

"Well, I suppose this one night at this exact time I had to," I answered, sounding more annoyed than I meant to. "Jeffrey," I said, trying not to acknowledge the awkward space that Dottie has put between them. I gave him a polite nod, and he returned it with apprehension.

"Good evening, Henry," Jeffrey said through gritted teeth. "I imagine you don't usually get your shopping done this late all the time. Do you?"

I knew exactly what he was asking. Are we going to run into you again? "Oh, no," I assured him, holding up my free hand in surrender. "Just this once. I had some last-minute errands that-" I paused to chuckle at this most unfortunate circumstance. "I suppose just couldn't wait 'til morning."

"We were only out this late to avoid all the after-work traffic," Dottie explained. "Sometimes, Jeffrey and I do our shopping together to save time."

I nodded at her, not wanting to know why she felt the need to explain herself to me. Unfortunately, her message was all too clear. I could feel myself growing more and more uncomfortable standing in the silence of the fight yet to come between Dottie and Jeffrey.

"I'd better be on my way. It was good to see the both of you," I lied, quickly taking my leave. They both answered in unison that they were glad to see me too, but I knew we were all dreading that moment together.

I purchased my produce with expediency and welcomed the brisk night air once again as I trotted down the sidewalk with my paper bag. I wondered to myself what the point of all of this was. Why did I feel like I was suddenly being punished? Why had Opal not written to me in so long? Why did being in love suddenly feel like such a burden? A rock settled itself in the pit of my stomach, and I could feel myself growing sick. This side of love was a foreign concept to me. For a split second, I wondered if all of it was even worth the fuss.

“Philippians 4:13,” I whispered to myself as I traced the sidewalk's edge nearing my apartment. “I cannot do this alone.”

Chapter Thirteen

Henry

Two weeks seemed to pass in a blink of an eye, and still, no letter arrived from my darling Opal. I prayed for her wellbeing every day. Wondering why she hadn't written was more torturous than anything I could have conjured myself. I tried my best to hold onto faith. I knew God must have been testing me. He must have been testing my patience to see if I truly loved her, if I would wait patiently for her. I knew that I could and that I always would.

I decided to busy myself with work and study to distract myself from thinking about my next visit to the post office. I was finally starting to get somewhere with my union research and knew it was time to take action on a plan.

One Tuesday morning while we were bringing in a load, I had my first go at recruiting with Chip and Ives. Ives didn't seem to mind my rants, but Chip was painfully quiet for a gentleman as outspoken as himself.

"Wilbur Dudley has been gone for over a month now with no pay or promise of a job when he's healed," I said, reminding them of what they already knew. I knew the recent incident with the Wilbur fellow injuring his foot was already causing uneasiness to many of the workers. Everyone was tediously careful with every move they made while on the dock. Using Wilbur as a prime example to start my campaign could very well be how I would get a foot in the door with the dockworkers. "That poor guy could have been any of us."

Ives continued to mark things down on his clipboard. He nodded, but I knew he was more so humoring me than agreeing with me. Chip didn't breathe a word. He worked on in silence, never letting on if he was interested in the things I had to say. I pressed on anyhow, as these gentlemen were great practice for me. "Ives, don't you still have family back in France that you send money to once a month? They rely on that income. Don't they?" Ives' eyes darted to mine from his clipboard. His eyes were hard at first, daring me to say anything further. Then, seemingly after a moment's thought, they slowly softened, and he let out a knowing sigh. He reluctantly nodded at me, returning his focus to the task at hand. I pressed on. "And, Chip-"

"Watch it," Chip gritted through pursed lips. I recanted and thought through my next statement. I decided it was worth it. After all, I was looking out for not just my job but all of ours.

"Weren't you just telling us that your mother is sick and can't afford her doctor's visits?" Chip's eyes widened at my boldness.

"You're way outta' line, Viefhaus," he blared, taking what seemed like giant strides toward me now. I continued anyway, even though I was growing more intimidated by the second.

"Wouldn't it be nice if you could pay for her health insurance?" Chip's strides picked up, and he was almost to me now. "Or even better, what if she could be placed on your insurance through your workplace? With a union, you very well could." Chip was right in front of me now. He was only an inch taller than I, but his anger seemed to make him grow an extra foot or two.

"I know your type, Viefhaus. You gotta have the attention, and you gotta have it now," he challenged. "Don't you ever bring my mother up to me again! This union shit you're trying to start ain't gonna change a damn thing." This was the angriest I had ever seen Chip. He was usually the jokester, but I suddenly realized that Chip did not like me. I knew I had never done anything to him, but something about me ticked him off. I could see it now. "Keep me out of your little plans. I hear you talk about this shit again, and I'm taking it to Ranger." He walked away without a second glance.

I made a mental check in my mind that Chip was not on board. Ives, on the other hand, just needed more time to form his own opinion on the matter. I was shocked to notice Ives was still checking inventory on that damn clipboard, even after that brief encounter with Chip and me. He hadn't even given Chip's dramatics a second glance. I chuckled to myself at the unnecessary heat of this uncomfortable moment and nodded my head at Chip's request. "Alright. I'll behave if that's what you want."

The other dockworkers proved to be just as difficult to win over. I knew I couldn't bring up the matter in broad daylight with supervisors overseeing our every move. Instead, I waited until I saw someone take a smoke break and approached him when he was away from inquisitive ears.

My first attempt was with a worker named Jerry Lewis. He was a total breeze to pitch to, and for a brief moment, I prayed that all the pitches could go this smoothly. Although, I anticipated they wouldn't. I explained to Jerry how a union could provide job security, as well as better pay and working conditions, and he was practically begging me to go on. I was pleasantly surprised by his transparency as he explained to me that he's been having back pain since he started this job. His doctor recommended he take two weeks off of work to recover. Jerry worried that, after the Wilbur incident, anyone could end up on the chopping block. He wouldn't dare ask for even a day's work off. He doubted there would be a job for him to return to if he did. I thanked Jerry for his time and told him that I would be in touch with him.

The other gentlemen were not so easy. I spent my entire lunch hour outside the restrooms, waiting for workers to come out so I could talk with them. During the first ten minutes, I babbled on and on to a burly man named Todd Wentworth, who kept his curly brown hair covered with a dingy, worn cap.

"So, you're saying that I'd have to have a portion of my paycheck go to these so-called union dues, just to be a part of some club?" He chuckled at me and shook his head. "Move along. I'm not your guy."

"We could eventually make changes to remove those dues, but while we're establishing this union, you must understand there will be costs to cover the upstart," I clarified, practically chasing behind him as he strode away.

"I said move along, Viefhaus!" he bellowed without so much as turning around. I sighed and turned back to my post, almost too defeated to press on.

After a seemingly useless lunch hour, I made my way back to my dock. On my way, I passed by Herman's dock and decided to pay him a quick visit.

"Henry! What brings you to the west port, brother?" Herman beamed, jumping down from a wooden crate and wiping his hands against his trousers.

"Just thought I'd drop in before I finished my lunch," I said glumly.

"Why the sad expression, Hank?" Herman could never be in a happy mood if he knew someone else was down. I shook my head and forged a smile.

"Oh, it's nothing. It's just that trying to get people to get on board with this union is harder than I anticipated." I complained, but I knew Herman could turn my spirits. He always had something positive to say. But strangely, in this moment, his expression seemed to harden, and he crossed his arms like our father did when he was preparing to lecture us.

"Tell me, Henry. Is this union thing really important to you?" Herman questioned.

"O-of course! It's how I'm going to afford to get Opal down to California. It's how I'll ensure that I can always provide," I answered, wondering how he could even ask such a thing. Herman's jaw involuntarily clenched as I spoke. He tossed my answer around in his head before replying.

"I gotta tell you, Henry." He sighed and willed himself to tell me the truth. "I-I don't think this union thing is such a good idea right now. I mean, Ranger's been looking for any excuse to fire workers." I felt my face drop a little as I gathered myself from the shock of this moment. After all these weeks of studying and preparing, I come to find out my brother didn't even believe in my cause.

"Herman, you can't be serious?" I countered. "How could it possibly be a bad idea when it would bring job security to every man on this dock? So that people like Mr. Ranger couldn't just do a round of firing whenever he pleased."

Herman shook his head and exhaled a little, doing his best to tiptoe. "You'd be willingly putting your job on the line, Henry, and for what? A woman you haven't seen in almost two years?" At this, my mouth dropped open. Not only did he not believe in my cause, but now he was telling me that he didn't see my courtship with Opal as legitimate? "I know you care about this Opal girl and all, and I suppose that's what matters. But it just seems risky is all I'm sayin'."

"You think I'm doing all of this simply because I care about Opal?" My voice was calm and grounded, but I could feel it steadily rising.

"Henry, don't be so quick to get offended. I-"

"You think I'd waste a second of my time expediting this cause when we all know it's inevitably going to happen?"

"You can't know that, Henry. Why do you have to be the one to take that risk?" he argued.

"Herman, you can't be so ignorant as to think that a union won't ever establish itself at some point in time. New York and most of the east coast have already implemented union. How much longer do you think it's going to take before the same system reaches our shores?" I could feel my blood growing warmer. "It's foolish to believe there could be any other outcome." I could tell my words struck a chord with Herman, but I was too preoccupied defending myself to care.

"You dare question my intelligence because I look out for you, brother?" Herman shook his head at me in disappointment.

"I can assure you. I am not pressing this issue simply because I care for Opal," I snapped back at him. "You think I'd do any of this for some dame when she's nearly two thousand miles away?" I pointed a finger at him. "Opal is everything to me. She isn't just some woman that I can forget about; she's going to be my wife!" I shook my head at him in disgust. "I'm sorry you can't understand that. I'm sorry you gave up on Grace Christian, but I'll never do that to Opal." I saw Herman's fist ball at his side. I knew I had gone too far, but the words just kept tumbling out. "You're angry that I'm doing what you were too afraid to do."

"Fine." Herman put his hands up in surrender, and I could see his skin reddening with anger, his jaw tightening every second. I could see he was fighting every instinct to knock me square in the jaw. "You want to screw up the best job you've ever had - a job that I broke my back to get you, let's not forget, over some girl from back home?" He stepped aside and motioned for me to pass. "Go ahead. I won't stop you. But don't you ever use what happened with Grace to validate your decisions to me again. You have sunk lower than I thought you were capable of stooping, Henry." My stomach twisted at his words. Herman gave me one last vengeful glare and walked back to his station.

I stormed back to my dock and let the heat of my anger energize me. I got more done in three hours than I usually got done in a whole day.

After the day was over, I didn't bother searching for Herman on the dock. I decided to skip the bus ride home and found myself taking a much-needed silent walk into town. I knew I'd apologize to Herman eventually, but now I was angry. I wanted to sit in it a while.

I crossed the street into *Point Fermin Park* and found an empty bench by an overhanging tree. The chirping of the distant birds seemed to be the only occurrence happening. Sitting felt good. Doing nothing felt good.

"Well, I suppose I'm the last person you'd hope to see these days."

I closed my eyes and prayed that the familiar voice I'd heard could belong to Herman or one of the guys from the dock - anyone besides whom I knew it was. I glanced to my right only to find Jeffrey Waters approaching my exclusive bench, hat in hand. Thankfully, he was alone. I chuckled at the sky in wonder of my misfortune.

"Well, you're not the very last person. I suppose," I said, shrugging a shoulder and sliding over so Jeffrey could sit. "Dottie. She'd be the last person just about now." I laughed arduously. Jeffrey gave an understanding laugh in return, which was far from what I had expected of him. There was a pause between us. I imagined neither of us had expected to see the other in the park of all places. "You know-" I started. "Regardless of whether or not you'll ever believe me, I feel it's important that I tell you once and for all that I do not have feelings for her. She was a friend at one point. Now I think even that has faded."

Jeffrey nodded genuinely. "I've made my peace about you, Henry. I have no desire to punish you unjustly." The sun seemed to glow a little brighter at Jeffrey's kind words, and for the first time today, I could breathe a little easier.

"Thank you, Jeffrey. It's a relief to hear you say that." I sighed, thankful to know it was finally over between him and me.

"May I ask you something, Henry?" Jeffrey fidgeted with his hat and focused on the glare from the sidewalk, careful to avoid my gaze. I nodded, approving but said nothing. "Well, Dottie's uh- I mean, she's probably one of the most beautiful women I've ever met." I smiled a little to myself as I watched him struggle to find the words. "She's so headstrong! A lot of men wouldn't be too keen on that quality in a woman, but I find that it makes her even more irresistible to me." He babbled like a giddy boy in his youth with a crush. "An-and she practically threw herself at you, Henry!" He shook his head in disbelief. "I mean if I had a shot, a real shot, with a woman like that… we'd be married by now and expecting our second child." Jeffrey continued to shake his head, unbelievingly. "Forgive me for my blunt approach, but what is the matter with you?"

I respected Jeffrey's honesty, not just about me but about his feelings for Dottie. I pulled a pipe from my inner pocket and took a match to its brim. "I respect your asking, Jeffrey." I puffed on the stem a few times to get it started. "I've never been able to look at Dottie that way. I have feelings for another, and I intend to marry her as soon as I can master an honest way to live." Jeffrey's eyebrows stretched up to his hairline. I let out a steady stream of smoke and nodded at his shocked expression.

"You? Henry Viefhaus, in love?"

"Is that so difficult for you to believe?"

"No, no, no." Jeffrey corrected. "It's just that. You seem so stoic is all."

I considered this interpretation of myself for a moment. I had never imagined myself as stoic, reserved, maybe - but stoic? "It's possible you just don't know me well enough, Jeffrey," I answered, and the silence blanketed between us once again.

"Does Dottie know that you're involved with someone else?" Jeffrey tried to sound casual in his inquiry.

"Yes. I've talked about Opal many times before with her."

"She's never mentioned that to me before." Jeffrey's insecurities were beginning to show, and I realized it was time for me to take my leave.

"Well, it's the truth," I answered, rising from my place on the bench. "Thank you for talking with me, Jeffrey. This was pleasant." Jeffrey nodded from his seat but spoke no words. A puzzled look was all he could offer as I dismissed myself and headed back into town.

I arrived home to an empty apartment around six. Herman was likely spending time with Millie or blowing off steam somewhere. We hardly ever fought, but when we did, his temper was always far worse than mine.

I stretched out across my bed and stared up at the ceiling of my bedroom. There was a crack in the corner that I hadn't noticed before. My eyes wandered, searching for other things I may have missed. I spotted a small cobweb forming in another corner of the ceiling and a dark, scuff mark on the wall near the door. It was interesting to see how many little things I had missed or even forgotten about just in this one room.

A sudden realization struck as I remembered the small box my father had mailed to me months ago. It had been sitting in my nightstand since I'd moved in with Herman. I leaned over the side of my bed and slid open the bottom drawer of the stand. Sitting neatly untouched was the small cardboard box. I quickly removed the package from its hiding place and studied the words on the postage. August Viefhaus, my father, St. Louis, Missouri. I remember being anxiously awaiting the arrival of this one small parcel. Now I've nearly forgotten it in an attempt to ease my anxiety.

You'd better not lose it, Henry. Your mother would have a field day if anything happened to it. My father's words rang in my ear as I rushed to the kitchen, box in hand, to find a knife to open it. I quickly cut away the twine that held the flaps of the tiny box in place.

At first glance, the inside only seemed to have crumpled paper inside. I knew that could only have been the work of my mother, trying her best to protect the precious cargo that lay within. After removing an unreasonable amount of tissue paper, I finally found a white handkerchief folded neatly at the bottom of the box. The initials H.V. had been sewn on the corner in navy-blue cursive. I'm sure my mother was the culprit behind the embroidery as well. It was a nice touch. I thought to myself.

Carefully, I pulled the handkerchief from the bottom of the box and placed it in my palm. I gently ran my thumb up the center of the cloth until I felt it, a small lump, hidden between the folded handkerchief, barely visible from the surface. I carefully unwrapped the handkerchief in my palm, mindful not to move too quickly. Layer by layer, the small cluster beneath the surface began to grow more visible as I peeled back each corner until sitting perfectly and untouched in the center of my palm, was a diamond ring.

It ain't much, but it's still a fine inheritance, my boy. My father's voice echoed again. *Find yourself a wholesome girl, one that you can be proud of.* Opal's beauty struck me like a train, and I imagined her sweet little hands bearing a ring that would tell everyone she was mine. The thought of Opal's recent silence came flooding in, sparing no mercy to my insecurities. Perhaps she was growing tired of waiting. Maybe an engagement ring could break her silent spell.

I took a deep breath, beaming at the stone before me. It seemed to only radiate in my hand as I balanced it in my palm.

I suddenly felt an impulse, one that I had been too afraid to acknowledge before, but it was clear now. It was time for a proposal.

Chapter Fourteen

Opal

"Mind the margins, Nettie. Hettie, Laverne is spelled with an E at the end." The twins were sitting at the kitchen table early this Saturday morning while Mama fussed at them. The poor girls were inescapably shackled to the kitchen table as Mama hovered over them and barked out her orders as they hand wrote invitations for the Laverne-Pleasant wedding. They were likely to be making cards all day if Mama had anything to do with it. Mama had been so excited about my acceptance of Thomas' proposal that she made a wedding announcement in the paper, calling our union "The Wedding of the Year." Thomas told Mama and me to spare no expense while we planned; he said his family was more than proud to pay for this glorious event.

My best friend, Laura, and I were busy planning all the details of the big day. We had set up shop in the living room and had lists for everything: guests, flower shops, tailors, restaurants, and everything else in between.

"I can't believe you're going to be Dr. and Mrs. Laverne. How elegant!" Laura doted as she held up two squares of lace pattern to the window for light. I rolled my eyes at her and feigned a smile. "You must be positively thrilled!"

"I suppose," I said indifferently. I crossed off a name from the 300-person guest list. I was in the process of trying to narrow it down to 150 people. Laura cocked her head to the side, confused.

"You suppose? Well, don't you know, Opal?"

"Yes, of course!" I replied, attempting to patch up my solemn tone. Before Laura could ask another question, there was a knock at the front door. "I'll get it!" I declared, taking my opportunity to escape.

I opened my front door to find two well-dressed, young, blonde women about my age, beaming at me from the other side of the screen door. One had her hair cut short into a neat bob with finger waves that were so perfect; it looked as if she were wearing a wig. The other had longer, shoulder-length hair, and wore it curled and pinned back to accentuate her features.

"Hello, are you Opal?" The short-haired girl asked through the screen. Her voice was higher than expected, but it sounded like she was trying to make it squeak on purpose.

"Yes. Can I help y-"

"My goodness! Well, aren't you just darling?" The short-haired girl answered before I could finish a sentence. The two girls screamed as they invited themselves in and wrapped their arms around me.

"I'm Coral Laverne, and this is Daisy Laverne." She pointed to the long-haired girl as she sized me up. "We're Thomas' baby sisters, and we're here to help you plan the perfect wedding!"

"It's going to be spectacular!" Daisy squealed as the two girls jumped up and down in my foyer.

"Well, what's all this?" Mama said, wiping her hands with her apron as she entered.

"We have guests," I said, still settling from the surprise visit. "Mama, these are Thomas' younger sisters, Coral and Daisy Laverne." The two Laverne girls curtsied and quickly removed their coats. Before I knew it, Laura and the twins had come to see who was creating such a ruckus.

"Your house is so... quaint," Coral said, eyeing the corners of the ceiling and exchanging a look with Daisy. She gave a polite smile and grinned at Mama.

"Yes, Mrs. Pleasant. You must be so proud of your modest house on the corner," Daisy cut in. "And who knows, perhaps one day, after Opal and Thomas have married, you might be able to sell it and enjoy something bigger that will suit all your needs." Coral shot Daisy a glare and gave Mama an easy smile.

"What Daisy means is, our family is more than happy to pitch in with this wedding and anything else you may need in the future." Mama nodded, seemingly able to decrypt every word they were saying. She smiled politely in return and motioned for them to follow.

"Well, won't you come in girls? Any kin of Thomas is kin to us!" I watched Mama attempt to fix herself, quickly removing her apron from around her waist and smoothing her hair, which had been pulled back neatly behind her head. "You've come on the right day, girls. We've been making arrangements all morning."

The girls linked arms and followed Mama into the kitchen. I watched their eyes wander around the small space with contained judgment.

"Perhaps you two girls could help Opal and me. We've set up shop in the living room," Laura said in her mousy voice, prying their glances away from our scratched kitchen table.

"I'm sorry, dear, and you are?" Coral asked.

"This is Laura." I cut in. "She's my closest friend, and she'll be assisting with all of the wedding arrangements."

"Oh, well, of course!" Daisy laughed. "We are so pleased to meet you." Daisy curtsied as Laura and I led the two of them into the living area to show the Laverne girls our progress. Mama's sour expression just barely escaped their eyes as we freed ourselves from the awkward tension of the kitchen.

"Laura and I only have the colors and the guest list decided as of now. I'm still attempting to narrow it down quite a bit," I said, as the four of us settled on the paralleled couches. I picked up the three pieces of paper I had managed to scribble all of the guest names on and handed the list across the coffee table to Coral.

"Oh, nonsense!" Coral chuckled, amused. "Darling, this wedding is going to be immaculate. We're going to want as many guests as possible, so everyone knows it's a Laverne event." Daisy nodded at Coral in agreement.

"We Laverne's throw the best parties!" Daisy said, smiling.

"Oh," I answered shyly. "Well, I suppose I was only trying to be mindful of the budget. It would be improper to spend so much when it isn't my family's money. I guess I can discuss it with Thomas."

"No need to ask Thomas," Daisy answered. "We'll take care of it. Now tell me, what are your colors?"

"Well, my favorite color has always been blue, same shade as the sky. We could accent all of the table settings with a nice powder blue and add small hints of gold-ish yellow. My bouquet could be sunflowers with gold and blue ribbon wrapped around the stems. And we could even-"

"Sunflowers?" Coral's lips pursed like I had said something profane. "Powder blue and yellow? No, no, no. That won't do. We were thinking of something much more elegant."

"Imagine this," Daisy went on. "Red roses everywhere, each seat at the ceremony could be decorated with roses. The flower girls could drop rose petals before you enter. And your bouquet!" Daisy placed the back of her hand to her forehead pretending to faint. "Oh, darling, it would be to die for! The stems could be wrapped in white pearls."

"And then at the reception," Coral added. "All of the centerpieces could be accented with roses and tied with beautiful red bows." She squealed and clapped her hands together. "I know a place in town that sells the most beautiful ribbons! At the end of the night, when it's time to see the bride and groom off, instead of rice, we could all scatter rose petals at your feet. Oh, it'll just be stunning!"

"Oh, what a beautiful idea, Coral!" Daisy cut back in, not allowing me to even get in a word. "Yes, I'd say that red and white should be your colors. It's by far the most classic look."

The two sisters nodded at each other with accomplished looks drawn on their faces.

"Well, perhaps we could have powder blue and gold at the ceremony and red and white at the reception," Laura added in her mousy voice. I smiled at her, happy to see she was trying to keep the peace.

"Oh, no!" Coral tried hard to add a polite smile to her pointy glares, but it was no use. "We can't mix colors. The wedding would be an absolute spectacle!"

Laura tensed at Coral's remark, too shy to push back. The rest of the day seemed to carry on similarly. As Laura and I presented our ideas, one by one, the Laverne sisters shot them down. I did my best to comply with them. I knew one day they'd be my sisters-in-law, and I didn't want to cause trouble so early on.

Mama checked on the four of us several times, always catching a catty remark just as she exited. I could tell she didn't like how Coral and Daisy behaved, but all the same, she never corrected them. She was likely doing the same thing as I was, trying to keep the peace.

"So, Opal, tell us. Aren't you just thrilled to be marrying Thomas?" Daisy asked while we worked on the seating chart for the reception. By this time, we had moved to the formal dining room.

"Not if it took her this long to give Thomas an honest answer," Coral mumbled under her breath. It was just loud enough that I couldn't pretend I hadn't heard it. Daisy elbowed Coral, who immediately looked up shocked, realizing she'd spoken out loud. Daisy raised an eyebrow at Coral, prompting her to fix her mistake. Rebelliously, Coral rolled her eyes and huffed while holding a fake smile. "Well, it's true. No sense in lying about it."

"I can assure you that I am very excited to marry your brother," I blurted, trying to save us all from another awkward moment. "The only reason I took so long to say yes was that I like Thomas so much. I wanted to make sure we got to know each other well, and I wanted both of us to fall in love." The Laverne girls said nothing. The painful silence had begun.

"Honest, I think Thomas is just swell!" I added. Coral rolled her eyes; she had completely given up on being cordial.

"So, Opal," Daisy started, trying to break the stiffness. "Tell us how many children you would like." She beamed a genuine smile that I knew I couldn't trust.

"Well, I've never had an exact number," I lied. I had known from the time I was ten years old that I wanted to have two girls and two boys. The problem was I never imagined their father to be someone I didn't care for. "I suppose I'll have to discuss it with Thomas."

Coral turned her nose up at this answer and smirked. "By the time I'm engaged, I intend to have everything planned," she said with pride. "I'll know how many children we'll have, where we'll live, and even what our family traditions will be."

"Once you're engaged?" Daisy laughed at her sister. "Good heavens, I know all of those things now! I've been planning my wedding from the time I was seven years old. What kind of woman would I be if I wasn't?" Coral nodded at Daisy's remark in agreement.

I had had just about enough of the Laverne sisters and their snarky comments. Future sisters-in-law or not, I was not going to let them degrade me any longer with their backhanded comments.

"Well, I'd say being in a relationship is much different than the fantasies we women can create in our heads," I said smugly. "Surely, if you've been courted before, then you'd know exactly what I'm talking about. A real man is so much different than the ones we read about in romance novels, wouldn't you agree, Laura?" Laura nodded at me with pride, happy to finally have the upper hand. The Laverne sisters' mouths gaped open almost in unison. "Have either of you been courted? I'm sure women of your social status should have men lined up at your door. Am I right?"

I could hear Laura trying to contain her laughs. The Laverne girls may have been bred into a wealthy inheritance, and they were pretty enough, I suppose. But their attitudes made them ugly.

"I-I've been courted by plenty of suitors." Daisy stammered. "It's just that none of them ever came close to winning my affections or meeting Daddy's standards is all." She turned her nose up at me, clearly offended.

"And so have I," Coral added. "I simply prefer to keep the relationship private is all."

I nodded at the girls, who were undoubtedly lying, and shrugged my shoulders at them. We worked another half-hour in complete silence until Mama finally saved us with her loud presence.

"Opal, dear," Mama said, stomping her way into the dining room. "I just realized the invitations don't have dates because you never gave one to me. I need your final wedding date. What is it?"

"February eighth," I replied as I drew a circle on a blank piece of paper to plan another table setting.

"Thank you, darling." Mama exited as quickly she came, clicking her shoes down the hallway and back into the kitchen.

"Dear Lord, February eighth? Do you intend to make Thomas an old man before you marry him?" These were the first words Coral had spoken in a half-hour, although with her shrill voice, it didn't seem long enough.

"February eighth is such a long time away. What reason do you have to put it off so long?" Daisy asked.

"Ladies," I said, putting my hands up in surrender, although my tone was less surrendering and more so annoyed, "that's less than a year and completely reasonable for a wedding this size."

"Oh, please," Coral scoffed, "it's completely improper to wait so long with a man so eager to marry you, especially after such a big announcement!"

"Yes, my concerns exactly!" Daisy encouraged. "The entire town will expect a wedding within a couple of months. Do you intend to drag this out so long for nothing other than dramatic effect?"

"I'm sorry, but Thomas has already agreed. February is set," I said as politely as I could. The two girls huffed in unison but avoided arguing further with me. "I must say. I don't quite understand why you're so anxious to rush. Plenty of people have yearlong engagements, and mine is only nine or ten months at the most." Coral rolled her eyes at me but refused to answer.

Daisy carefully weighed her next words in her head before finally speaking up.

"Well, it's just that our brother Thomas is much older than you are," she said carefully. "And our father has already put a great deal of pressure on him to marry as quickly as possible. Daddy wants Thomas to start a family very quickly after you are married. You know Thomas is nearly thirty. Don't you agree that he needs to start having children?"

I nodded, understanding. I hadn't considered the position that Thomas was in being a man nearly thirty years old and still never married. "I suppose I can understand that," I sighed, "but to be honest, girls, I'm not quite sure that your family is even very fond of me. They don't even know me that well yet. Do you want him to marry so soon without any knowledge of my background?"

"For heaven's sake, do you know what type of wealth you'll be marrying into?" Coral snapped. "Forgive me, dear, but what else is there to consider? We don't need to know your family's background because, well, let's be frank, there isn't much to know." She said in a fake polite voice. "And as for our family's background, it's money! Problem solved. Now we can move on to discussing the actual wedding date. Ninety days. That's all we need to plan the perfect wedding." Coral stood from her chair and reached for her purse at the corner of the table. "I'll talk to Thomas about it tomorrow. Come, Daisy. I wanted to go for a dip in the lake, and I'm already growing tired." Daisy stood as well, and the two girls collected their things.

Laura and I walked the two sisters to the front door and gave polite grins to them as we closed the screen door behind them. Laura exhaled relief once the door closed, and I realized that I had been holding my breath too as we watched them leave.

"Oh, dear, Opal. They are simply awful!" I nodded at Laura in agreement and huffed. "Oh, well," she continued. "Luckily, when you're with the right one like we are, nothing else matters. Right, Opal?" She gave a positive smile and squeezed my arm as she trailed down the hallway and into the kitchen.

"Right," I said, with a knot in my stomach.

Chapter Fifteen

Opal

I felt myself beginning to worry if anything I was doing was even worth it. Every letter I sent to Henry and every word he wrote in return all seemed to trickle down into nothing as I sat on the front porch that early morning holding my left hand up to the sun's rays, trying to steal a better glimpse of the blue sapphire ring that Thomas had given me.

I wondered if perhaps Mama and the Reverend were right. Perhaps love would come. Maybe one day I could grow to care for Thomas, and possibly Henry would fade into a distant memory that didn't make me ache with every passing thought. I suppose, when I considered it, Henry had abandoned me. I can still remember the day he told me he was going to leave St. Louis to pursue a career in California.

We were attending Laura's New Year's Eve party at her home, just four houses away from mine. Every local soldier in town had been invited per Ralph's request. Ralph and Laura's love was still but a budding rose, but it was apparent that their feelings had taken root.

Henry and I were supposed to go to the New Year's party together. However, a few hours before, Henry stopped by the print shop to inform me that he'd have to meet me there due to private family affairs. Annoyed, I agreed to meet Henry at Laura's. I even thought it was a better arrangement seeing that Laura would undoubtedly need help with preparations.

People began arriving around seven o'clock. Laura and I managed as well-to-do hostesses reasonably well as we ushered the guests in and hung their coats.

Hours seemed to fly by, and Henry still hadn't arrived. I was beginning to believe that he wouldn't come at all.

"Opal dear, where's that handsome beau of yours?" Odette Stedmond was coming right at me from the kitchen. Even with a crowd as large as this one, she had managed to single me out in the formal dining room. I let out a sigh at my misfortune as she approached me, offering no more than a dainty hiccup. Odette was balancing her wine in one hand and a long cigarette holder in the other. I never much cared for Odette. She was one of those girls that was far too opinionated and much too flirtatious around the men. "Have you bored that poor Henry with your sob stories already? So, your father died, like no one else's has." She tripped over her heel and spread her arms out to her sides to steady herself.

I rolled my eyes at her and allowed her drunken opinions to roll down my shoulders and crash to the floor. "Oh?" I said with more poise than I thought I was capable of. "Well, I suppose you would be the expert in men growing tired of you. You seem well practiced in the sport. I must say." Odette's face scrunched into a sour expression of shock and anger. I couldn't believe my boldness. Although, I think it partly came from the knowledge that Odette would likely forget the entire conversation by the morning once she'd sobered up.

"Pity," she said, reclaiming some of her dignity. "If he had come, perhaps I could have allowed him to entertain a real woman, one who isn't afraid to let a man be a man."

"And I suppose lying on your back with every Jack, Steve, or Harry makes you a real woman?" I snapped back with confidence. I could have done a cartwheel. I was so proud of myself. Odette never bothered with a reply. She took her leave silently and gracefully, searching for her next poor fellow to victimize.

The rest of the party seemed to go along just fine, except that Henry had yet to show his face. I was beginning to worry that something terrible had happened.

"Ten minutes until countdown!" I heard Ralph blare as he stood by the fireplace with a glazed over expression. All the guests cheered. Their simultaneous roars seemed to vibrate the outer walls of Laura's house, and I suddenly was very aware of how full her home had become. I had tried to keep track, to control the mess, but somewhere along the way, I lost control of the crowd of people. Laura was no help. She fawned over Ralph all night, never letting go of his arm, not even for a sip of water. Ralph pulled Laura in and kissed her lightly. I rolled my eyes at the sight and made my way through the crowded halls until I reached the front door.

Once outside, the cool night air quenched my dewy skin, and I felt my shoulders relax. I looked down the road a bit, hoping to catch my Henry pacing his way to me, but the dirt road was silent and empty.

"Fiiiive Minuuuutes!" I heard Ralph bellow from inside. The whole house seemed to be in an uproar over the announcement.

"Hello, Darlin'!"

I spun around in hopes to see Henry's shining face headed my way. To my disappointment, it was just a drunken guest. I believe his name was Larry or Lewis, something with an L. He staggered towards me. I took a few steps backward, so he wouldn't run into me. He lit a cigarette and tried to steady himself against Laura's mailbox.

"How ya doin', sweetie? You out here all alone?" He involuntarily burped and clutched his chest. I waved my hand in disgust, trying to fan away the smell.

"Ugh, you're drunk. Why don't you go back inside, will ya?" I said, annoyed.

"Can't, doll," he said, taking a puff from his cigarette. "Ralph kicked me out. It would seem the prick doesn't know what it means to have a good time." I suddenly recalled him being very flirty with Laura, and I immediately understood.

“Perhaps you can be of service, doll. You look like you know how to have fun.” He looked me up and down and smirked.

A shudder came over my shoulders and trickled down my spine. “Well, I’d better get back inside. The clock is ticking,” I said, taking my leave.

“Off so soon? We haven’t even gotten to know each other,” he said, reaching for my arm. I quickly pulled away.

“I suppose you’ve gotten to know each other plenty.” I heard a firm voice say. I spun around to find Henry rushing towards us from up the road.

“Henry, dear, you’ve nearly missed the whole party. Where have you been hiding?” I asked sweetly, although my undertone was annoyed.

“Sorry, darling. I had a meeting, and I lost track of time,” Henry said, taking my hand and leading me away from the drunken man. The man didn’t seem to care. He rolled his eyes and puffed on his cigarette as he stumbled down the dark dirt road.

“Should we make sure he gets home alright?” I asked as our fingers interlace.

“Leonard’s a smart fellow. He’ll find his way,” Henry said as we settled onto Laura’s front porch swing.

“Tell me, what kind of meeting lasts until this late into the evening?”

“The kind that offers me the career opportunity of a lifetime,” Henry said with eyes lit wide.

“Career opportunity? I thought you wanted to take over your father’s farm when he retired.”

“Opal dear, this is far more of a promising future than tending a run-down farm.”

“Well, what is it? Who is this businessman that’s got you all riled up?”

“His name’s Jeffrey. He came into the drugstore while I was picking up my father’s prescription. I noticed how dapper he was dressed, and we got to talking. Apparently, he’s in town for a cousin’s wedding, but he resides in California.”

“California?” I said, sounding more alarmed than I meant to.

"He's offered me a job working as a desk clerk for a newspaper printing company."

"In California?" I asked, this time feeling truthfully threatened. Henry nodded as he beamed at me.

"That's right! I leave in two weeks," Henry said, practically bubbling out of his shoes. I could feel my heart sink deeper with each passing second.

"You're leaving for California in two weeks?" I suddenly had no oxygen and was in desperate need of air. He nodded and brought my left hand up to his mouth and kissed it.

"Unfortunately, I won't be able to take you with me when I go. I'll need time to find a place and get settled in. Once I've made enough money to provide for a family, I'll send for you to come and join me. We'll marry and start our lives." Henry's tone was so calm and sure. I turned away from him and gripped the underside of the bench with all my strength, taking in deep breaths to keep from crying.

"Well, how long do you suppose it will be before you'll send for me?"

"It's hard to say. Perhaps ten, eleven months, I suppose."

"Twenty! Nineteen! Eighteen!" We heard the mob from inside roar as they counted down the New Year. It seemed they were also counting down the seconds to my journey of sadness as well.

"Eleven months?" I replied, standing from the bench. "You want me to wait for an entire year before we can be together? Do you realize how much can take place in a year?"

"Sweetheart, there's no need to panic. Surely you understand that I'll need time to make a decent living for the two of us."

"I hear the women are far less modest out there. However, I suppose you've already thought about that," I sassed.

"Opal." Henry pleaded, looking disappointed.

"You're going to be on a beach somewhere in California with bare-legged women prancing around you! And then you tell me that you're going to send for me in a year?"

"Darling, please don't upset yourself." Henry stood and wrapped his arms around me. I pushed him away, even though I wanted nothing more in that moment than for him to hold me.

"You're not going to be thinking of me in a year. I'm sure by then you'll have moved on with some pretty blonde."

"Opal, honey, what do you suppose I'd be doing all day? Sitting in a cafe, preying on women until sundown?" He chuckled to himself. "Darling, that's absurd. I'll be working hard for us. My brother Herman is already living there, so any free time I have, I'll be spending it with him. I will marry you, Opal Pleasant. You are going to be my wife." Henry attempted to wrap his arms around me a second time. I pushed him away again, this time involuntarily.

"I don't believe you," I said. As tears begin to fall, I made my way down Laura's porch steps.

"Nine! Eight! Seven!" the party boomed in unison.

"Opal, please just hear me!" Henry called.

"If you wanted to end things with me, there were far simpler ways to do it besides running two thousand miles away," I said through sobs as I ran down the road.

"Two! One! Happy New Year!" I heard the house faintly roar as it grew further behind me in the distance. I kept running. I didn't know where I was headed. I needed to be alone. I passed my home and decided to keep running. I just kept running.

Chapter Sixteen

Opal

The post office was empty when I arrived. Leroy toyed with a deconstructed pocket watch. He seemed focused, so I decided not to greet him. I found a blank piece of stationery and an ink pen sitting on a counter-height table in the back of the post office. I didn't know what I wanted to say. I had this overwhelming sense of peace that everything was going to be alright.

St. Louis, MO
June 10, 1929

Henry, My dear, sweet Henry.

It has been torture not to talk to you, not to write to you, my love. But I knew telling you the truth would be far more painful. I know you have wondered where I've gone. My love, I can assure you that I am alright, dear one. But Henry, I'm afraid I have less than pleasant news to share with you.

I have agreed to marry Thomas Laverne. I couldn't put him off any longer. Mama and the Reverend Stone were giving me such grief about it that they wouldn't accept no for an answer. Oh, Henry dear, I feel completely isolated. How I wish I could run away to be with you. How I wish marrying you was much simpler than all this. I don't want to give up on us. If you don't write back to me after reading this, I'll understand. But I pray to God that you will. I love you dearly, Henry.

Opal.

A tear-stained the paper as I folded it neatly and stuffed it inside an envelope. I hid away in the corner of the post office until I could dab at my eyes to keep the mascara from running. After collecting my thoughts, I stepped back into view and approached Leroy, who was cleaning the cogs of his opened watch with a handkerchief.

"Haven't seen your cheery face in weeks. Good to see you, Miss Pleasant!" Leroy said as I approached the counter.

"Oh, yes," I replied politely. "I guess I've had a lot to do at home."

"I suppose that's true! Congratulations on your engagement," he said with a smile. "I read about it in the paper a few weeks ago. *Wedding of the Year*, eh?" Leroy winked at me and laughed. I giggled sweetly and pulled out a nickel for postage.

"Could I please have the key to my box. I'd like to check if I've gotten anything lately."

"Sure! What was your box number, one-eighty-five?"

"One-seven-five," I said with a smile.

After Leroy had distracted himself with his watch once again, I found my way over to the post office boxes. I stared at the small metal plate on the outside of my box with those three worn numbers on the front. I knew if I didn't bring myself to open it then, I never would.

I jimmied the key into place and quickly turned it. With one swift motion, I opened my mailbox to find four letters stuffed inside. The sight of them sent my nerves into a frenzy, and I fought hard to retain the feeling in my legs. I removed them one by one and read the name at the top of each one. All of them belonged to Henry. Guilt crept over my shoulders and wrapped itself around me.

I quickly pulled the letters from their hiding and locked the box door back into place. I tore open the first letter and allowed Henry's words to wash away all my anxieties.

He loved me. Even still, he was waiting for me patiently. I opened up the second one to find myself relieved again at Henry's sweet words. I could hear his voice so clearly. Every word bounced off the paper and made sweet noise against my eardrums.

I anchored myself in a back corner of the post office and read the last two letters. I allowed my smile to reach my ears as I laughed at Henry's contagious positivity, even after all he had been through.

I was lost in the pages. I read them each two and three times over, trying to remind myself that he was real. Henry was real.

Two brothers, one sister, and a cat, I heard Henry's voice say, clear as day in my head. A memory that traced all the way back to my third date with Henry began to reenact itself in my thoughts as I hid behind a card stand.

Henry had taken me to a local park for a picnic. We were walking through the grass, trying to find the perfect place to lay out our blanket. Henry was trying to guess how many people lived in my home.

"Two sisters, no cat, and the sisters are twins," I said coyly. Henry snapped his fingers and howled.

"Darn, so close!"

"You were nowhere near close!" I giggled.

"I don't suppose you've got a dog instead, do you?" I shook my head at Henry and smiled. It was the first time I remember myself feeling comfortable with him. The first time my heart wasn't fluttering with anxiousness, and I could think clearly.

"I thought that was you, Opal!" I was pulled out of my memory to find Mrs. Colt from the print shop walking towards me.

"Mrs. Colt! What a pleasant surprise to see you here," I lied.

"Enough of the nonsense, girl. I don't like being spotted in public any more than you do." She rolled her eyes. I chuckled a little at her candor. She was never one to shy away from speaking her mind. She approached me and sighed as she reached into her purse, pulling out an envelope. "I was in here to mail this to you, but since you're here, I'll just give it to you personally."

"What is this?"

"It's your final paycheck," she said coldly.

"I'm closing the shop. I've got to move back home to take care of my skeleton of a mother. She's nearly ninety years old, you know?"

"You're closing the shop? What am I supposed to do now?"

"I figured it wouldn't matter now that you've got that rich fiancé to take care of you. I saw your wedding announcement in the paper."

"My mother did that," I said, surprisingly saddened by the news.

"Well, if you ask me, I think it's just plain classless, announcing a wedding in the paper as if it's as important as world news." Mrs. Colt shook her head and scoffed. "You young people are really somethin'."

"Where did you say you were moving to?" I asked, hoping she would say somewhere in Europe, far away from me.

"California," she said as she buttoned her purse. My heart took a leap as I heard the words.

"How did you end up in St. Louis?"

"Ugh," she grunted, waving her hand to shoo away my inquiry. "That's neither here nor there. All I can say is never leave your home for a gent you're not married to. You never know how the real story will turn out." My chest caved in as her words struck a chord. Without warning, every emotion I'd been feeling suddenly hit me all at once. Tears welled in my eyes, and I was fighting to keep them from dripping onto the new dress that Thomas bought for me. Mrs. Colt rolled her eyes and huffed. "Oh, for heaven's sake, child. What is the matter with you?"

Mrs. Colt was the last person I'd wish to see me this way. Unfortunately, she had to witness an unplanned breakdown in the back of the post office. Mrs. Colt pulled a handkerchief from her coat pocket and handed it to me with annoyed concern. I took it and quickly dabbed at my eyes as the uncontrollable sobbing began to take root.

"Alright now, child. That's quite enough. Get ahold of yourself and tell me what's the matter." She crossed her arms and waited for me to calm myself.

"Mrs. Colt. If you had the choice, would you marry for love or money?"

Mrs. Colt's expression soured as she let out a sigh and rolled her eyes. "You listen to me, young lady. I don't know what you've gotten yourself into, but I suggest you put a stop to it right now. Thomas Laverne is a doctor, and it would be foolish of you to ruin such an opportunity. The Laverne family is very well known and respected here in St. Louis."

I nodded, trying to both appease her as well as convince myself that she was right.

"In the beginning, love is not a factor. If a man is willing to take care of you, it is your job to let him. Love comes after years of marriage; it is never immediate. You hear me?"

"Yes, ma'am," I said, dabbing at more tears.

"Whatever mess you're in, fix it." She snatched the handkerchief from me and replaced it in her pocket. "And do it quickly."

"Yes, ma'am." Before I could say any more, Mrs. Colt vanished from the post office, leaving me in my misery.

Chapter Seventeen

Henry

The letter was short, not even a page long. Opal explained her engagement to Thomas Laverne in less than a few paragraphs.

"Eyes on the rigging, Viefhaus!" Chip said with a hateful tone.

Lately, we had been working double time on the docks. Mr. Ranger had accepted a large account with a shipping company in South America. The new account had almost tripled our workload, but Ranger was refusing to hire any new hands to divide the work.

I pushed Opal's letter from my mind and got back to work. It was harder than I expected to drain my thoughts of her. All I could imagine was that slimy doctor trying to win over her affection.

"Twenty-nine," Ives said with a smirk as he approached with a clipboard in hand. He had been secretly recruiting fellows on the North and South docks to join the cause for a union. I had managed to win over Ives after speaking with him at length about how being a foreign citizen made it more likely that he would be the first to go during a season of layoffs.

"Beg your pardon," I said, giving him the signal to keep his voice down when discussing union establishment around Chip. Chip was still refusing to get on board. Had the person fighting for the cause been anyone besides me, he might've already joined. Chip seemed to loathe me irrationally.

"I count twenty-nine men from North Dock who have signed the petition."

"What about South Dock?"

"That is not so easy," Ives said, shaking his head. His French accent revealed itself strong and unapologetic. "The men of the South Dock have Chip as their influence. They do not want anything to do with your cause."

I sighed annoyed. Chip's incessant need to undermine my every move was rapidly growing old. I couldn't figure what would drive him to spend such immense energy on bringing my downfall. "Alright," I said, defeated. "Do we have anyone from the South Dock?"

"One," Ives said shaking his head.

"Not enough," I replied, shoving the clipboard into Ives' chest and walking away. Immediately I caught myself and turned to him. "I apologize. I'm just exhausted." Ives nodded his head with understanding.

I decided I'd try my hand at South Dock during my lunch. I was hoping to spread some fresh perspective on the matter. After all, a union was for the benefit of everyone. How foolish would you have to be to pass an opportunity like this one up?

"Your union is a load of horse shit!" a burly man named Gary said as he spat a large ball of saliva into the dirt. I stood before twelve South Dock workers as they ate their lunch on benches a couple hundred feet from the docks. At once, the workers all erupted in laughter at Gary's comment, and a few of them even cheered. I felt like a schoolteacher trying to teach children the importance of eating their vegetables. Sadly, they were having none of it.

"Gentlemen, please," I said, putting my hands up in surrender. "A union means better work environments, paid time-off, decent wages, and health insurance. These are things we could all benefit from."

"So how you figure we'll be making more money if your union would take ten percent of e'vry dollar we makin'?" Charles, a young buck who was just recently hired, said. He couldn't have been older than seventeen, and he had a southern accent that gave him away as soon as he opened his mouth. A few fellows nodded at him, and one even patted him on the back.

"The union dues would only be to ensure that we keep the union running. It would need funding of some sort. We could even discuss lowering it to eight or nine percent once we get it off the ground."

"How about zero percent?" Gary shouted with a piece of salami shooting from his beard-covered face in the process. Everyone laughed and clapped, cheering as if the comment were the most brilliantly constructed joke anyone had ever told.

"If we keep our heads focused on the immediate sacrifice, we'll only hinder our future!" I shouted through the erupted laughter.

"What are you, some kinda preacher?" asked a short man with curly dark hair. I was pretty sure his name was Jenson. Once again, everyone howled at my expense. Jenson got up and stood before the rest of the men. He folded his hands and bowed his head, pretending to pray. "Let's all say a prayer for this unfortunate soul who still doesn't get it!" Again, laughter filled the benches. I shook my head, annoyed, as Jenson continued to make gestures like he was an ordained minister. Some of the men were holding their sides from laughing while others shook their heads at Jenson's reenactment.

I walked away, clearly defeated but mostly frustrated that these workers could let someone like Chip persuade them away from something good for them.

The remainder of the workday was long. I worked the rest of my shift with full force as Opal's letter rang in my head all the livelong day. I tried to escape her words with hard, sweat-bearing work, but it was of no use. My Opal had promised herself to another man. Whether or not she had been given a real choice in the matter didn't change the fact that hidden underneath my anger was pain. She had said yes.

After work, I instinctually stopped by the post office. I wasn't sure why I still did this. I knew Opal was likely not writing another letter. Still, I found myself yearning for her words. I wished to console my agony with her thoughts and bandage my wounds with her stationery, stationery she would have just touched only days before I would.

When reality reclaimed my daydreams, I saw that Opal had not sent me another letter. She hadn't written again to say that she'd refused Thomas' hand and that she could only be with me. I reached for a pen. I allowed myself to do something in which I had not done before - to doubt.

San Pedro, CA
July 23, 1929

Dearest,

By the time this reaches you, I suppose you will have already begun planning your wedding arrangements to Thomas Laverne. I suppose you'll have the wedding right there in St. Louis, the place you've called home all your life.

If memory serves me, St. Louis is also where you, several years ago, met a young man. And since, he has grown to love you devotedly. And even though far away, he is loving you still. Honey, how I would love to see you tonight. How I would enjoy one of those wonderful evenings of your beautiful love and companionship. Remember, dear, the many wonderful evenings that we have spent together. How I often wonder and remember those moments when I could just lean over close and whisper, I love you. Those were the days of real genuine happiness. Yet, I never realized it then as I do now.

Now all I can do is recycle thoughts in my mind of how my love was not enough. Your hands are not in mine. I cannot find your lips nor you in my arms. I've realized that just as I am in agony, so you must be. I have received your letter regarding your betrothal to Thomas.

I cannot lie to you and say that my heart is not aching for you a little more this night. I long to feel your love at close range, your kisses and the smiles that made me so intensely happy once upon a time. I am steady counting the days until you can be my wife. Yet, it saddens me to know that even in this moment, you are counting the days to become a wife to someone else, to Thomas. I cannot tell what is real anymore. I see you here, right here in my arms as mine, as my own. But when I blink my eyes, you are nowhere to be found.

However, even in my sadness, I will not withdraw my request for your hand. I cannot rescue you from your current state, Opal. But I deeply pray that you will find a way to end your arrangement. My heart is heavy, and I do not know what the end will look like for us. But I am choosing to hold onto God amidst my doubt. I will pray for your well-being.

Sincerely yours,

Henry

My soul felt numb as I folded my letter and encased it in an envelope. It felt as though I were giving up, as though I were giving Opal up. I did not like the idea of surrender, but at this point, what was my choice? I had none. I left the post office in a hurry, hoping that no one would spot me in my sunken defeat.

Herman was entertaining Millie when I arrived home. He had the record player set to a beautiful jazz instrumental, and the smell of marinara sauce was thick in the air. Herman's head was hung low over a steamy pot on the stove. Millie sat on the couch, seductively might I add, and puffed on the stem of her long blue cigarette holder.

"Henry! I didn't expect you to be home so early. Hadn't you planned on going to the library tonight?" Herman said, finally pulling his head out of the steamy pot. He gave me a look that I interpreted as him wanting me to leave as soon as possible. I nodded and hung my coat on a hook by the front door.

"I had, but I'm quite exhausted now. I suppose I'll be turning in early tonight," I said, heading for my room. I turned to give Millie a polite nod. "Pleasure to see you, Millie."

"You as well," she said right before blowing a perfect smoke ring. I pretended not to see and quickly locked myself in my room.

Outside the door, I can hear Herman and Millie's muffled conversation. I couldn't make out the words. Still, judging by the cadences, I assumed Herman was apologizing for my unexpected interruption in their evening. Herman and Millie had been growing closer by the day. I had never seen my brother so happy, so in love. Well, not since Grace Christian.

Grace Christian, or as most people liked to call her, Herman's saving Grace, was Herman's first love. They met for the first-time volunteering at a shelter for the homeless and less fortunate. Grace had been there on her own volition. Henry, however, was doing mandatory community service as part of his plea deal for partaking in a bootlegging drop-off that went south.

Herman loved Grace more than anything in his life but was still young and wasn't exactly keen on settling down with Grace so early. He wanted to marry when the time felt right, when he had gotten a little older and was making decent money. My pa urged Herman to ask for Grace's hand, but Herman insisted that Grace understood his desire to wait until they were older. This went on for over a year. Then one day, seemingly out of nowhere, Grace paid a visit to our farm, which was odd for her, seeing as how our farm was so far from the inner city. Grace insisted that she needed to speak to Herman in person.

In the middle of our wheat fields, Grace proceeded to tell Herman that a wealthy man from France had asked for her hand. He was going to take her back to France and give her a lavish life, the kind of life a girl like Grace deserved. Grace admitted that she had accepted. She told Herman that if he asked for her hand right then that she would deny the Frenchman her hand and stay to be with Herman. But Herman was stubborn and hurt. He told Grace if she could accept the offer of another man, then she should go and be with him.

Grace left our fields a hysterical mess. I had never seen a woman cry with such passion. But Herman wouldn't budge. He wanted to punish her for his pain. Three days later, after grueling hours of my pa and I attempting to persuade Herman to go and make things right with Grace, he finally agreed to ask for her hand. My father gave Herman our grandmother's wedding ring to take with him. When Herman went to Grace's house, her father informed him that Grace had already left for France two days prior.

I had never seen Herman so miserable. He was not himself for months following his heartbreak, and I prayed every day that God would never allow Herman to go through such pain again. And he hadn't. But here was Millie, and it seemed Herman was really falling for her. Doing things for her, he hadn't done for a woman in years, things he had only ever done for Grace.

I laid on my bed, forcing my eyes shut and willing sleep to come. I heard Millie burst into laughter at something Herman had said from the kitchen. I sighed and squeezed my eyes tighter now.

"Please, let sleep come," I whispered to myself. "Please."

Chapter Eighteen

Henry

"So, it seems you and Millie are going pretty strong these days," I said, trying to get an idea of Herman's thoughts about her. He shrugged coyly as we headed towards the pier early that morning to begin our day.

"Wouldn't you like to know, brother?" Herman smirked as we finally made it to the docks.

"I suppose, by now, the two of you are pretty exclusive?"

"Exclusive is quite the word choice I'd say. It's more like we're figuring one another out."

"But you like her, right?" I tried my best not to sound too eager.

"Well, I suppose. What's not to like? I mean she's no canceled stamp, and I guess I really like that in a woman. I like a woman that's got a fiery passion in her. You know, perhaps one who's not too shy on tellin' me when I'm full of shit once in a while when I need it." Herman nodded his head and chuckled, approving of his own assessment of Millie. "Yeah, Millie's a great girl."

I could see the joy in his eyes when he spoke about her. Immediately my concerns about this girl seemed pointless, and all I could feel was utter joy for my brother. We proceeded to stamp our timecards and headed toward the docks.

The dock was in full action today. We had two unexpected shipments come in from Columbia on top of the regular workload we had anticipated. There was no time for recruiting today. Ives kept his head down with his clipboard in hand while I tried my best to manage through the grunt work without annoying Chip.

Around noon, the sun seemed to be beating down hotter than it had yesterday. Sweat dripped from every area of skin not protected by my clothing. I was loosening a rope atop of a boxcar when I realized my thirst and the heat of the day was finally more than I could bear. I jumped down from my post and hid behind a part of the boxcar that was shaded from the sun. I fanned myself with my cap and tried my best to catch some cool air in my mouth.

"The hell ya doin', Viefhaus? Get back up there!" Chip growled with the husky voice he had specially reserved for me.

"I need some air. It's strikingly hot today," I replied, not in the mood.

"You think we don't all wanna take a break and fan ourselves underneath the shade? You got some nerve, like you're the only one working hard around here."

"Not now, Chip," I groaned, losing my patience. "Haven't you grown tired of this routine? I'm fed up with your grumbling on about nothing. Leave me be."

"You got a problem, Viefhaus?" Chip started puffing his chest into mine.

I put my cap back on and secured it into place, careful not to break eye contact.

"Let's say that I do. You seem to have one with me. I suppose that's your prerogative, so I reckon I do as well," I barked, with more anger than I realized. I'd blame my lack of patience on the heat of the day, but Chip had been pissing me off for weeks. He deserved whatever he had coming to him.

"You're bold," he said with a laugh. I didn't return the gesture. I could only stare at Chip with what must have been pure hatred in my eyes.

"And you're a cheap shot," I declared, puffing my chest in return. "What else you got?"

"Henry, don't," I heard Ives say from a few feet away.

"I think you oughta listen to your friend, Viefhaus," Chip said, smiling in a low, raspy voice.

"So, you've finally managed to get a thought to cross your mind, eh?" I taunted, shrugging my shoulders. "Must've been a lonely journey, I'd imagine."

And with that, we were off. No longer words were in between us now, only fists and at times a worried Ives, desperate to break us up. Chip thrusted me backward into the boxcar, and I could feel a bruise forming as soon as my spine made contact with a metal ridge. I wasn't going to let him win that easily. I gripped two fist-sized handfuls of his shirt and forced him backwards. We released each other almost simultaneously. We brought our fists up, ready for something we'd both been looking forward to for months.

"Henry, please! Stop this at once!" I could hear Ives shouting, but I ignored him and took the first swing. Chip ducked in anticipation and came back up just in time to connect with my jaw. I could taste blood and saliva pooling in the left side of my mouth and was livid, far past the point of no return. I went in for another swing, this time more calculated, and managed to knock Chip square in the cheek. He stumbled backward a step or two but hardly seemed affected. Chip took another swing at me, and I managed to recoil just far enough to miss it but close enough to feel the wind behind his fist make a swift breeze against my cheek. So close, I could feel the hairs on my cheek stand up.

I charged at Chip and tackled him to the unforgiving, wooden-planked floor of the dock and pinned him down with all my strength. I manage to throw in another punch - this time connecting with Chip's nose, sending blood everywhere. I went for a second swing and made contact with his cheekbone, just below his left eye. I hoped to God that it left a nasty bruise.

Simultaneous to my punch, Chip threw one back at me and knocked me square on my lower lip. He drove his fist inward as forcibly as he could, and I could feel my teeth cut the inside of my mouth as my bottom lip molded itself into an unnatural cast around my bottom teeth. I pulled back and tried to refocus my attention, this time aiming for Chip's gut.

Before I could drive my elbow down into his unguarded stomach, I was suddenly overtaken by four, maybe six, possibly even eight hands, all gripping at my shirt and pulling me backward off of Chip and onto my feet. My rage took over, and I tried my best to escape these interrupters, as I was nowhere near finished with Chip. I took another charge at him just as two men helped him to his feet. However, I realized my chance was over as the forceful hands again found their way to my chest, pushing me backward with a firm grip.

"Enough!" Herman shouted, eyes digging into mine. He looked almost as angry as I was. I suddenly realized that he was one of the men pushing me away from Chip. "Take a walk, Hank!" Herman pointed inland toward the shore.

I abruptly came to and remembered where I was. I looked over at Chip and saw that he now had three men holding him back. I knew he could easily break free of them had he wanted to. The fight was over, and we both knew it. Chip's left eye was swelling quickly, and a purplish hue was already darkening beneath the socket. His nose was also slightly crooked, and blood was streaming from both nostrils. I wondered to myself if I could have possibly broken his nose. I couldn't recall feeling any bones cracking when I smashed my fist into the bridge of his nose. Then again, I couldn't recall much of anything that had taken place just moments before.

I nodded at Herman in agreement and took my leave, furiously making my way inland. Once on land, I found the nearest restroom and locked myself in. I went to the sink and gathered large scoops of water in my palms to rinse my swelling cheek. I caught a glance of myself in the mirror as I was rinsing and saw that my bottom lip had swollen to twice its size. Besides the lip, I could see no real sign of having ever been punched. I remembered how badly Chip's face looked in comparison to mine, and it made me smile. If we were judging by damage done, I was clearly the victor. I reached for a paper towel and soaked it with cold water and pressed it to my aching lip. The coolness of the towel soothed the pain, and I sighed as I realized my job could be on the line for this.

Once out of the restroom, I found a nearby bench in the sand and decided I deserved a moment to sit. Pressing the wet towel against my lip, I closed my eyes to enjoy the rare breeze that passed through.

"Henry dear, what on earth has happened to you?" The familiar voice sent my eyes blinking wide open to find none other than Dottie herself clicking her heels towards my bench. She was wearing a beautiful red dress with a matching red beret and holding a shimmery red cigarette holder, which she puffed as she gazed upon my face in horror.

"Dottie," I said, quickly rising to my feet. I could feel my swollen lip beginning to hinder my speech. I had to hold it in place with the towel to speak. "What brings you here?" I asked, halfway pleased to see her and halfway annoyed that of all days to visit, she'd chosen this one.

She wrapped her arms around me in a somewhat comforting embrace and squeezed. I winced, realizing now that my spine was quite sore from when Chip rammed me into the boxcar. I waited for Dottie to sit on the bench before finding a seat beside her.

"Oh Henry, this new job must not be right for you, dear. Look at you - you're all black and blue!" Dottie said, pouting with a motherly tone. "Who's done this horrible thing to you?"

"I'm fine. I'm just fine," I replied, waving my hand to dismiss her worries. "What in the world brings you out here? Is something the matter?" I realized more and more how unnatural it was for Dottie to pay me such a surprise visit, and I began to fear the worst.

"Oh, of course, everything's alright. You've got no need to worry about little ol' me," she said reassuringly, though I could sense the doubt behind her tone.

"Well then?"

Dottie sighed deeply and began to tap her foot anxiously. She caught me eyeing her twitch and held her leg still to keep it from shaking.

"You've never come to the docks before," I said, my voice cool but my head running with possibilities of what brought her.

"I just don't know how to say something like this to you, Henry!" Dottie cried, almost instantly bursting into tears.

I sat forward, waiting for Dottie to confirm that the worst had happened. I recalled a faint memory of Dottie once saying that her father had extreme health issues on our way to the office one morning. Perhaps he had passed, and Dottie had no other friends to turn to. Dottie always struggled to make girlfriends. Women never quite took to her bold and somewhat promiscuous personality. I patted her shoulder and tried my best to be supportive, but my best efforts to comfort her were to no avail.

"There's no need to cry, Dottie. Tell me what's happened? What's brought you to such tears? Is it Jeffrey? Has he done something?" Despite my most recent encounter with Jeffrey and how progressive our conversation was, I found myself rising to anger once again at the mere thought of him.

"Oh, I shouldn't have come!" Dottie sobbed, shaking her head. "I shouldn't have come here. You have no ties in all this mess."

"Try to calm down, and tell me what's going on," I said firmly. Dottie tried her best to collect herself. She pulled a handkerchief from her purse and lightly dabbed at the corners of her eyes. She straightened her posture and let out a calm, collected breath. It seemed almost instantly that she had been cured of her hysteria.

"Jeffrey-" she started.

"I knew it," I said, gritting my teeth.

"Now hold on there, Henry," Dottie said, putting a hand up. "Jeffrey… has asked for my hand."

I was suddenly at a loss for words. What was I to do with this information?

"Jeffrey wants to, wants to marry you?" I chuckled, somewhat relieved and slightly mortified by the idea of it all. "I suppose that is terrible news," I laughed out loud. Dottie cracked a smile, seemingly to humor me. "Dottie, you're a woman who can't be tamed," I finally managed to say through eased laughs.

"Don't let something like this upset you. I'm sure you've found pleasant ways to refuse offers before. Haven't you?"

Dottie shook her head at me, and her sympathetic smile turned to a frown. "Henry, I've accepted."

I felt my cheeks melt into a similar frown. I stood from the bench and paced a little to think.

"You've accepted," I said, surprised by my disappointment. "You've accepted to marry Jeffrey?" Dottie nodded from the bench as I continued to pace. "Well, that's alright. I'm sure we'll find a way to get you out of this," I assured myself. I had a brief flash of five years ahead, and I pictured Dottie and Jeffrey making a home together, Dottie serving Jeffrey's dinner every night, wearing an apron, becoming a dutiful wife. It all seemed so unnatural it made my head spin. "You don't have to do anything you don't want to, Dottie. I assure you; we'll get you out of this."

"Henry," Dottie said with hesitation unlike herself, "I'm carrying his child." Her voice cracked as she struggled to get the words out, covering her mouth in an attempt to keep from crying all over again.

"Jesus, Dottie! You're pregnant?" I shouted at her, throwing my wet towel to the ground in an unforeseen temper. She flinched at my anger, surprised to see my reaction. "No, no, no," I said, throwing my hands up in surrender, "I can't bother with this." I walked away hoping to leave behind this nightmare that has become a living, breathing reality.

"Henry, please, I was hoping you of all people would understand!" Dottie cried, rushing after me.

"How would I understand?" I turned to face her. "Tell me, Dottie. Why are you telling me this, huh? What does it matter if I know - why must you keep interrupting my life?"

Dottie recoiled at my statement, shock and hurt painted plain as day on her face. "Because I want you to stop me!" she finally responded.

"Stop you from what?"

"Any of it, all of it! I want you to stop pretending that you don't see me! Please, Henry. I'm begging you to just look at me!"

"I do see you! You always come around. I see you everywhere I go!"

"Then, for heaven's sake, Henry, make me yours!" Dottie barked, nearly out of breath. We held our silence for what felt like hours. "You've been mine all this time," she finally said, in a voice that was clear and heavy. "From the day we met, I knew you were mine. You've been planted in my heart for so long. I can't remember what emptiness feels like." Her words struck me to my core as my heart broke for her. "I can feel it. Right here in my soul," she said, clutching her chest in anguish. "You are mine, Henry. Choose me. Make me yours, please. I beg you."

I was again without words for her. I had nothing to say to her. What was I to say to an engaged, pregnant woman on the verge of an emotional breakdown?

"I-I." Before I could find the words, Dottie raised a hand to silence me.

"I can wait a little longer," she said, in what seemed like an attempt to assure herself. She left and began to head inland. "But not forever," she countered, turning back toward me. She looked down at her stomach and grazed a hand across her still seemingly flat belly. "I suppose you've gathered that." She wiped a tear forming in the corner of her eye, and with those last words, she was gone, a spot in the distance. I noticed Dottie walking with slightly more caution like she had the whole world to protect.

Chapter Nineteen

Opal

"I wish you wouldn't be in such a hurry to leave me all the time," Thomas said, clasping my hands in his, eyes glimmering like a lovesick teenager. It was unlike Thomas to be doting on as he was. Still, I assumed he was in a chipper mood because his old friend Chester from medical school was in town on business. Thomas had been going on and on about how long it had been since he'd last seen his best friend, Chester.

We stood in Thomas' office, cotton swabs and strange medical tools surrounding us on all sides with an oversized desk right in the middle.

"I'm sorry, dear, but I must get going. Mama and the girls are planting lilies in the garden today. We're hoping they will bud in time for the wedding. Mama will be absolutely furious if I miss even a moment of wedding preparations," I said, gripping Thomas' hairless chin in my palm, attempting to be affectionate.

"I'll be seeing you later tonight, so it's just goodbye for a few hours at best," I teased, taking my leave.

"About that," Thomas replied, taking my hand and pulling me back toward him, "I'm no longer able to make dinner tonight with Reverend Stone."

I sighed, frustrated that he couldn't have told me earlier. "We've been planning this for weeks now. Reverend Stone is supposed to give us his blessing. Why didn't you tell me?"

"I'm sorry, dear," Thomas declared, patting my hand. "I completely forgot I have a meeting later with my old friend. You know the-"

"Sure, of course I do. Your old college friend is visiting," I said, cutting in. "I suppose I can try to smooth things over with the Reverend."

"You're amazing!" Thomas pecked my cheek. I nodded with a frown, partially annoyed at the inconvenience and partly relieved that we were skipping a meeting to have our relationship officially blessed by God.

"Well, I'd better get going. I don't want to be late."

"Actually, Opal, before you go, I have one last question I wanted to ask you." Thomas had a strange expression on his face that I couldn't read.

"Sure, what is it, Thomas?" Thomas clasped his hands together and perched himself at the edge of his desk.

"Opal, would you ever consider traveling abroad?"

"Abroad?" I asked. "Well, I've always wanted to go to Paris if that's what you mean. You're a fan of tourism?"

"No, no, no," Thomas said with a chuckle. "I was thinking more like Mozambique, Sudan or Somalia, something like that."

I must have blinked about a hundred times in three seconds. I had only ever heard of one of those places, and I wasn't sure they were the best places to vacation.

"Oh?" I manage to spit out. "Well, I wouldn't necessarily go on holiday to any of those places, but I imagine you've got a point to all of this?"

"I do," Thomas said confidently. "My good friend from school, Chester Whittaker, is part of a doctor's abroad program that allows doctors to travel to less fortunate countries and administer healthcare to people in need, who couldn't afford it otherwise. That's partly why I can't make tonight's meeting with the Reverend. I'm meeting with Chester to discuss the program. Of course, I would like to see how you feel about such a great endeavor. So, what do you think?"

"I-I don't know what I think," I stammered, realizing that my marrying Thomas could potentially take me further away from all the people I loved dearly, Mama, my sisters, Laura and of course, Henry. I knew the sentiment of it all was beautiful, and it wasn't until this moment that I realized how caring and compassionate Thomas was. Still, I found my stomach churning at the thought of being on a completely different continent than Henry.

"How long have you wanted to do this?" I asked.

"A very long time. Since my first year of medical school, Opal," Thomas said, squeezing my hands sincerely. "I know this is a lot to throw on you, but you have to know that this is very important to me. I believe it's my God-given destiny to fulfill. Whether you are to come or not, as your husband, I would ultimately decide. Though I would hope that you could find it in your heart to come willingly all on your own."

My heart sank at his words. He was right. There was nothing I could do. If Thomas decided we were off to heal sick children in a third-world country that was precisely what we would do. Thomas' office suddenly felt very small as I struggled to get any air in my lungs.

Just then there was a knock at the door. Before Thomas could answer, a tall man opened the door and peeked his head in to find Thomas and me inside.

"Ah, Chester! Come in. We were just finishing up," Thomas said with a wave. Chester walked in, and I immediately noticed how handsome he was. His broad shoulders and strong jawline were almost character-like. Handsome as he was, I couldn't help but notice that Chester seemed to be slightly older than Thomas, not by much, maybe a few years at most, but enough for me to tell.

"Chester, I'd like for you to meet my fiancé, Opal Pleasant, soon to be Opal Laverne," Thomas said, nudging me with a friendly smile. I tried hard to smile back although internally my heart was pounding, and I was terribly nauseous from the news I'd just received.

"Pleased to meet you," I declared as the panic finally subsided, and I could force myself to be cordial. I extended a hand out towards Chester, and he immediately grabbed it and kissed the top of it.

"The pleasure's all mine," Chester said with charming endearment. "So, you're the girl that's been keeping my friend all tied up these days."

"Oh, I hope I haven't been keeping him too busy," I laughed.

"Of course not. Thomas has said nothing but great things about you. You're his saving grace as far as I'm concerned."

I gave Chester a bashful smile.

"You're a little early, aren't you, Chester?" Thomas said, checking his pocket watch.

"Yes, I do apologize, but I wanted to get into town a little early for a meeting I'm having with Doctor Burkhart. We're discussing a drug that might be implemented soon. It's known as Penicillin. It's very new, but the rumor is it could completely change medicine as we know it."

"You mean that antibiotic created by Alexander Fleming?" I cut in. Both Thomas and Chester looked at me with eyes wide, likely shocked that I'd have any knowledge on the subject.

"That's right," Chester said with a smirk.

"I suppose I don't know much about medicine. I've read some of his work, and I think it's absolutely fascinating."

Chester nodded at me with both approval and bewilderment.

"You really did find the perfect girl. Didn't you, Thomas?" Chester declared. Thomas nodded, equally impressed.

"I suppose I did."

Once again, another knock at the door interrupted the three of us. We all turned to see Laura standing in the doorway.

"Laura," I said, happy to have an excuse to leave Thomas' office. "Well, I suppose I'll just have to catch up with you gentlemen later. I've got a thousand errands to run. Chester, it was great to finally meet you. Hopefully, we can get to know each other some other time."

"Of course!" Chester said happily. "Your husband and I are close colleagues. You'll likely be seeing a lot of me. I can assure you." A brief look of uneasiness registered on Thomas' face when Chester said this. He quickly hid it, but I couldn't help but feel a bit concerned for him.

"Well, enjoy your afternoon, boys," I said, pecking Thomas' cheek and finally taking my leave.

"I'll come by in the morning, dear," Thomas cried, closing his office door behind Laura and I as we linked arms.

Once outside, I finally let out a sigh of relief.

"Opal, who was that man? He was absolutely breathtaking!" Laura squealed as our heels clicked down the sidewalk.

"Oh, just a friend Thomas knows from medical school. Apparently, they've stayed good friends even after they graduated."

"Well, all I can say is the Missus must be very proud to have a fellow like that on her arm."

"Actually, I don't think Chester's married."

"Oh, thank God, there's still time!" Laura howled. I giggled at her ridiculous comment.

"Come to think of it, Thomas has never mentioned any special girl of Chester's," I shrugged. "Well, he is a successful doctor; perhaps he's particular with women. I mean, look at how old Thomas is, nearly thirty and just recently engaged to be married. Maybe it's a doctor thing."

"I suppose," Laura said, shaking her head. "Just seems a little unnatural for someone so dashing."

We took a few more strides before approaching Mrs. Colt's print shop. One of the many errands Mama had us running was for more paper, so we could practice making homemade flower bouquets out of tissue paper and bendable wire.

"You mind if we cut through the back alley?" I asked, as we got closer. "Mrs. Colt is rarely in front of the store, and I don't want to be waiting around forever."

"Sure," Laura said with a shrug as we cut through the back alley towards the print shop.

Just as we turned the corner to let ourselves into the back of Mrs. Colt's print shop, Laura frantically grabs my arm and points down the other end of the alley.

"Look!" she half whispered. I turned to see what she was referring to, only to see Thomas and Chester also standing in the alley a half a block away outside of his office. The pair were holding hands, and Chester said something inaudible. Thomas laughed and nodded. Before I could react to the hand-holding, Chester leaned over and planted a kiss square on Thomas' lips.

"Hurry, get down!" I said, grabbing Laura as we hide behind a trashcan.

Laura and I peered from behind the garbage can to watch with amazement. Chester hugged Thomas endearingly, and the two kissed once more. After a brief moment, Chester left walking down the alley and exited back onto the public street. Our mouths were gaping open as Laura and I watched covertly from a distance.

"Oh, my God!" I gasped, struggling to say anything else.

"I know!" Laura said, looking back at me with concern. "I guess that explains the no wife conundrum."

Chapter Twenty

Henry

I watched Dottie as she made her way back towards the city. I didn't take my eyes off of her until her silhouette was nothing more than a speck in the distance. Anxiety filled me as I thought back on our conversation just moments before. If Dottie was bold enough to be so honest about her passion for me, it was likely because she assumed that I'd respond with similar feelings. Guilt washed over me as I selfishly thought how I didn't have the time to stroke the ego of an unwed mother to be.

I forced myself to rid my thoughts of Dottie as I knew I had bigger problems to worry about, one being my swollen lip that Chip had so kindly given me just twenty minutes ago. I trudged back toward the docks, hoping to slip back into the rhythm of the workday without being spotted. If I could just get through this day, I knew things would turn around.

As I strode closer to the docks, I noticed that the mob of men that had all crowded around to watch my fight with Chip had still not dispersed. Among the crowd were Chip, three policemen, and an angry Mr. Ranger, spitting and cursing the air.

As I drew nearer, Mr. Ranger spotted me and stopped his rant to an officer mid-sentence to address me.

"And here comes the trouble maker now," Mr. Ranger yelled, shaking a fist at me. "You think you can cause havoc on my dock, boy!" He walked over to me and gripped a handful of my shirt. Two officers immediately responded by pulling Mr. Ranger off of me.

"Mr. Ranger," I said, realizing I was in deep water. "Mr. Ranger I-I didn't start this!"

"Well, guess who's damn finishing it?" Mr. Ranger said, attempting to charge at me again.

"Mr. Ranger, please let's try to be civil about this!" Herman pleaded, coming to the rescue and standing between the short angry man and me. Mr. Ranger glared at Herman with wild eyes.

"Cuff him!" Mr. Ranger yelled to an officer. Before I knew it, I was having my arms pulled behind my back as an officer wrapped handcuffs around my wrists.

"Sir, is arresting him absolutely necessary? The fight barely lasted a couple seconds," Herman pleaded.

"I don't give a rat's ass!" Mr. Ranger blared. "Get him off my dock!"

"Shoulda kept your head down, Viefhaus!" Chip howled with an evil grin as the officer escorted me to a police car. At this comment, Mr. Ranger whipped his head around and laid into Chip.

"It'd do you some good to keep your own mouth shut, Dunham! Matter of fact, officer, you can take him too." Chip's eyes widened at Mr. Ranger's betrayal.

"Mr. Ranger, you can't be serious? I ain't done nothin'! Henry started this whole mess with all his union-"

"I don't wanna hear it!" Mr. Ranger cut in. "Cuff him too!" An officer quickly approached Chip to cuff him as instructed. Chip tried to resist, and a second officer had to help the first as they forcibly wrapped Chip's arms behind his back. The officers swiftly escorted him to a second police car and tucked his head into the backseat.

"Let this be a lesson to the rest of ya!" I heard Mr. Ranger blare from the dock. "There'll be no funny business on my dock! I'm sick of this shit!"

The drive to the police station was brief. I could hardly concentrate on the trouble I was in as my mind only brought me back to one thing. How did I let this get so out of hand? My stomach twisted itself into knots as I realized I was losing any real chance of being with Opal.

Once at the station, an officer escorted me through the back of the building and uncuffed me. His badge read D. WALLACE in all capital letters. He sat me in a chair at one of the many desks crowded inside, took a short statement of the details of the fight, and then promptly brought me to my supposed home for the next twenty-four hours.

"There's a toilet in the corner. Don't holler 'less you're dyin'," D. Wallace said coldly.

"Wait. Would it be possible to make a phone call?" I said with forced politeness.

"You dyin'?" he asked, annoyed. I shook my head at D. Wallace's question. "Didn't think so," he barked as he swiftly turned and walked away. I sighed in frustration at the misfortune that had become my day. Never in a million years could I have predicted such an ending to an already horrific day. Yet, it seemed to only be getting worse.

Minutes later, after I had made myself comfortable on one of the cots in the corner, I was surprised to hear the gate to my cell opening with a creak. In the opening stood Chip, eyes cold, as an officer uncuffed him and shoved him inside with me.

"No, no, no," I said, quickly rising to my feet and clinging to the bars in protest. "You can't put him in here with me!" The officer spoke no words. He only eyed me as he locked the cell behind Chip and disappeared down the hall.

"What's the matter, Viefhaus?" Chip said, making his way over to the cot across from mine and stretching out. "Scared I'm gonna beat you senseless again?" Chip's legs hung over the bottom of the cot, as he was obviously much too tall for it.

I shook my head without warranting a response. I perched myself at the foot of my cot and closed my eyes, hoping the nightmare would fade away into nothing.

“Damn Ranger,” Chip said, turning to face the wall in an attempt to get comfortable in his tiny cot. I glanced over at Chip but decided not to reply, knowing he wasn’t actually talking to me anyway.

Instead, I sat and wondered about my dear Opal. I wondered what she could possibly be up to at this exact moment. She really was an amazing woman. Every part of her was good. I had never met someone so instinctively and inherently good like my Opal. I knew if she were the one in this prison cell, she’d set Chip straight in an instant. I could hear her sweet voice in my head. You oughta kill ‘em with kindness, Hank. If it were up to my Opal, she’d find a way to meet Chip right where he was at. Opal was compassionate like that.

In that instant, I knew I had to give Chip another go. If he wasn’t going to meet me on my terms, then I’d have to meet him on his. It was the only way to get the majority vote on the docks. With Chip’s influence, I’d have all the men I needed to sway the workforce in our favor.

“You think you being in here is some sort of accident?” I asked the back of Chip’s head, wondering if he’d even give me a response. He moved ever so slightly and let out an annoyed grunt. “Ranger would do this a thousand times over because he’s got all the power.”

“Can it, Viefhaus,” Chip mumbled. “Let’s just get through this night without killing each other.”

“I’m serious, Chip,” I press in, knowing I’m about to test my limits. “You think Ranger cares about putting food on the table for your two sons? Or that he worries about your mother’s heart condition?” At this, Chip turned over with rage in his eyes.

“You wanna get out of this cell so badly that you willin’ to die for it, boy?” I threw my hands up in surrender.

“I apologize,” I said with sincerity. “I’m only saying that Ranger’s job isn’t to look out for us. We gotta do that part ourselves.”

“You can stop your speech right there, Viefhaus. ‘Cause you ain’t never gonna see a dime from me,” Chip said, sitting up and leaning over as he spoke. It was a power play. He wanted to see if I would cower. I wasn’t about to give him the satisfaction.

"I know you don't like me," I said, "and that's all fine by me. But when it comes down to it, we gotta protect each other."

"I ain't got time to protect you none." Chip spat onto the cold concrete floor of the cell. "Like you said, I got a family to provide for. I don't need no ten percent being collected out of my paycheck for some silly club."

"I hear you. But this isn't some silly club. It's a way to secure the future that you want for your sons and all those medical bills your mother keeps stacking up? Imagine having the insurance to cover them."

"Dammit, Viefhaus! I won't say it again. You keep my mother's name out of this."

"Fair enough," I said, knowing nothing would change Chip's mind. "I know somewhere inside, you know that I'm right," I said, stretching out in my own cot and talking to the ceiling. "As long as the workers have no power, Mr. Ranger will always have the upper hand."

"Man, Mr. Ranger's sure got you bent, don't he?" Chip said, shaking his head. "You really believe I'd invest even a penny of my money into your petty vendetta for revenge against the man, huh? You think I don't got my own battles to fight?"

"Everyone's got hardships, Chip," I rebutted with a sigh. "So I suggest you do what you know is right, not just for yourself but for the men on that dock. If you don't and everything goes south, I hope you'll at least know who to point your finger at." With those words, I turned to face the wall, sure that at any moment Chip would either demand a second fight or tear me to shreds with a verbal lashing.

Instead, there was only silence from behind my shoulders. I could feel Chip's eyes burning a hole into my back as he surely must have been fighting to keep his composure. A few shuffles could be heard, and I sensed that his eyes were finally off of me. It wasn't long before I heard snoring from the other end of the cell, and I could finally relax.

I knew I couldn't wait any longer. Whether I had Chip's men or not, Mr. Ranger had to be confronted. I decided I would face him tomorrow with all the men in favor of the union proudly standing by my side. It was time we claimed our victory.

Chapter Twenty-one

Henry

We were startled awake after what felt like only a few hours. Chip and I both jolted from our cots at the sound of the prison guard's baton drumming against the bars of our cell.

"Rise and shine, boy! You got a visitor," the guard howled. Chip and I sluggishly rose to our feet.

"Who is it?" Chip mutters with a rasp.

"Don't matter. Ain't for you," the guard said as he motioned down the hall to someone we couldn't see from within our tiny cage. Seconds later, after hearing the patter of footsteps, Herman appeared on the other side of the bars.

"Herman!" I gasped, gripping his hands through the bars. I had almost forgotten he'd be waiting for me.

"Brother! How have they been treating you inside these walls?" Herman asked with an eased smile.

"Eh, it's not home, but it has served its purpose for the time being. How many hours has it been?"

Herman shook his head and sighed. "It's six am. You've been here since five-thirty last night."

"What happened after Chip and I were arrested?" I asked, cutting in, too anxious for small talk. Herman shook his head, guilt riddled on his face.

"Ranger says he's gonna tighten the leash from now on. He plans to make an example of you and Chip. Anyone who commits even the smallest of errors while working the dock will be fired. Ranger says that order needs to be re-established. Everybody's blaming you," Herman said with a defeated sigh. "It doesn't look good, Hank."

"That means I'm fired?" I said with a gulp. Herman's eyes immediately darted to Chip.

"I'm afraid you both are," he declared. At this comment, Chip lost all composure.

"You've caused me nothin' but trouble since you arrived," Chip said, storming from his backseat position over to me at the front of the cell. With one fluid motion, Chip gripped me by the collar and pushed me into the sidewall of our cell. "This is all your fault," he growled.

"Lay off!" I shouted. With all my might, I thrust Chip backward and forced him to release me.

"Both of you cut it out!" Herman shouted through the bars. "This is exactly why you two are in this mess!" Herman's yelling was deep and angry and was enough to bring Chip and me back to our senses. We backed away from each other but kept our eyes fixated on each other, prepared to start again at a moment's notice.

"There a problem down there?" we heard a guard from down the hall say. Herman glanced down the long hall, past where Chip and I were able to see, and apologized immediately.

"Sorry, officer, all good here," Herman said politely while Chip and I fixed our stretched collars.

"I can fix this," I whispered, approaching the bars to strategize with Herman.

"You wanna keep that pretty face. I suggest you speak up." Chip says, folding his arms and huffing.

"I said I can fix this," I said more loudly. "Herman, it's time," I said in a much more foreboding tone than intended. "If we want a union, we're gonna have to force it. Ranger's not gonna give it to us otherwise. I need you to gather the men."

"Which ones?" Herman asks.

"All of them. Everyone who supports the cause, all 52 of them. Every worker counts."

"Alright, what should I tell them?"

"Tell them there's no work tomorrow. Gather everyone on the docks at nine o'clock sharp tomorrow, but be sure no one punches in. Tell them we won't work until we get an answer."

"Henry, what you're asking for is job suicide!" Herman protested. "You can't expect the men to agree to this. Ranger would fire every last one of us. These men have families to feed, houses to maintain."

"They won't be risking anything if you can persuade all of the workers to sit out. Without a union, no one works," I said, feeling more sure of my plan the more I pieced it together. "Chip," I said, turning to him with pleading eyes and suddenly more open to a truce, "we need your influence."

"I bet you do," Chip said with a smirk.

"I'm serious, Chip. With your men, we'd have more than a majority of the dockworkers in protest. That could very well be the push that we need to win over Mr. Ranger."

"I think you're forgetting something, Viefhaus," Chip barked, clearly disinterested. "I don't want your damn union, and I ain't givin' you a penny of my paycheck."

"And I think that you've forgotten that you no longer have a job! If you want it back, I suggest you get on board," I fired back, fighting hard to maintain calm as I reasoned with him. "If we don't prove to the board that the treatment of the dockworkers is unfair and we need a union, you won't have a paycheck at all. Now, are you gonna continue being an ass, or are you gonna help us?"

Chip flared his nose at me, ready to charge. But before he could, the three of us were interrupted by an officer making his way toward our cell.

"Chip Dunham?" the officer asked.

"That's me," Chip's voice said with an air of exhaustion.

"You're free to leave," the officer declared, fumbling with a ring of keys before finding the one that would unlock ours. "Your bail was paid an hour ago, courtesy of your friends down on the docks."

Chip quickly collected his things and headed for the cell door with the escorting officer.

"Chip, please. I ask you to reconsider," I said, giving my last attempt. "If we all work together, we can protect each other."

Chip glared at me through the bars and spit on the concrete at my feet.

"Good luck," he said with a smirk before disappearing. Herman turned to me and pinched the bridge of his nose, stress washing over him from head to toe.

"We don't stand a chance without his extra men. Ranger will surely fire us all," Herman huffed.

Saddened, I returned to my pathetic cot and perched myself at the end of it, hoping that the answer would come to me.

"Time's up!" yelled an officer as he approached Herman and me. "He'll be out in a few hours. You can speak to him then. Let's go." The guard gave Herman a nudge.

"Herman, promise me you'll gather the men like I told you," I pleaded, rising to my feet once again. "Prepare them for a fight tomorrow!"

"I'll do what I can," Herman answered as he was escorted away. "I just don't see what good it'll do."

"Just gather the men!" I yelled to a now empty hallway. "I'll take care of the rest!" I declared, knowing I had no real plan.

Chapter Twenty-two

Henry

Hours passed, and before I knew it, I was released from my cell. It was now four in the afternoon, and my only mission was to make it to the docks before the men went home for the day. I knew I needed to prepare everyone for tomorrow. Thankfully the police station was just a few blocks away from the shoreline. I arrived at the docks by four-thirty. My one and only mission was to somehow make the impossible happen and get Chip's men to join the cause. I had no job, which meant I had nothing left to lose.

I spotted a group of men that I recognized as Chip's crew sitting together on a far-off dock on the west port. I counted eleven of them, laughing and chattering away before their shifts ended. I quickly made my way toward them.

It seemed I needed no introduction as their happy expressions turned to anger as they watched me approach. I chose to push forward in spite of my immediate intimidation.

"You lost, boy?" one of the men said, rising to his feet and dusting himself off. He was broad and burly, likely one of the alphas of the group. I quickly put my hands up as a sign of surrender.

"I'm just here to talk," I said, attempting to diffuse him. Slowly, one-by-one, they all began to stand to their feet.

"I think you done enough talkin'," the burly man declared. "I suggest you get the hell outta here before things get messy. You already cost one of our men his job."

"Please." I reasoned. As I began to speak, I noticed that other dockworkers had joined the circle. Slowly, as men began to trickle in from the docks to end their shifts, I found that my audience had grown sevenfold.

"I just want to talk to you about how a union can benefit everyone. With a union in place, Chip and I would have never lost our jobs. Ranger wouldn't be allowed to put in impossibly strict protocols whenever he felt like it. If we all work together to fight for this, we can ensure that we all have the job security that we deserve. Shouldn't we look after our own?"

"You mean like the way you looked out for Chip?" a younger gentleman challenged.

All eyes were on me at this point. I was quickly put on the spot, and I knew my next words would need to be chosen very carefully if I was going to win these men over. I took in a deep breath and closed my eyes.

"Final hour," I whispered to myself as I opened my eyes and exhaled. "Gentlemen." I began. "This is about more than Chip. This is certainly about more than two idiots getting into a fight while at work and getting fired for it," I said, pointing to myself. I got a few laughs from the growing circle of men, and it eased my nerves. I glanced around the circle, a crowd of about fifty men, and spotted Ives and Herman among them. I was relieved to see familiar faces among the crowd and felt a courage I hadn't known I possessed.

"If you're looking for a way to put food on the table tonight," I began, pacing my way around a circle that I had somehow become the nucleus of, "then a union is of no use to you. Go on and leave the circle now. Clock out for the day, as you are doing exactly what you need to be. However, if you're looking for a way to provide for yourselves and your families for a lifetime, then you'd better start thinking of how you're going to secure that future. Ask yourselves: What lengths are you willing to go to for your family? Do you have a secondary plan if this job falls through? Many of you would likely say no." Men began to shift uncomfortably as I went on. Their expressions changed from stubborn anger to intrigue.

"I came to California in pursuit of life, liberty and my pursuit of happiness, just as Thomas Jefferson said we are owed. When I first came to California, I was fortunate enough to find work rather quickly," I went on. "Securing a job so quickly gave me a false sense of security. I just knew that things were going to pan out just as I had planned them. I was determined. I told myself I'd save up for the first six months of employment and then send enough money back home to St. Louis for my gal to buy a train ticket and meet me out west so we could marry. But my good luck quickly changed. My former boss hated me and found the quickest excuse he could come up with to fire me."

"Sounds like you bring trouble ev'rywhere you go!" shouted a short bald worker from the sidelines. A couple people laughed, but I stayed the course of my speech. Soon, silence fell again.

"Within a matter of minutes, seconds even, I was at the bottom. I had to drain my savings, every last dime of it, to survive. I had to move in with my brother just to make ends meet. I was penniless and pitiful."

"Tell us something we don't know!" shouted a young fellow from Chip's crew. This warranted much more laughter, and I struggled to gain the men's attention once again. Even still, I progressed.

"Slowly, I dug myself out of the hellhole I was in. My brother Herman was kind enough to fight on my behalf to secure me a job here. I once again began to save up my money to bring my love out to California. All seemed to be right again. That is until yesterday. Once again, I am in battle, not just for my job security but for my life. A man's work is his livelihood, his bread and butter for conquering the world. What happens when that natural order is disrupted? My friends, even the Bible says that a man who does not work does not eat. Should it be deemed rightful that a man, with only so much as a title above ours, be capable of changing our destinies in an instant? Should men follow blindly into the darkness with no assurance of self-preservation? I stand here before you all to say that establishing a union isn't just about taking money from our pockets. It's about taking control of our own lives! Do we not have the right to life, liberty and the pursuit of happiness?"

"I'd say punching you might make me pretty happy right about now!" a large man from Chip's crew yelled, charging toward me. "I've had just about enough of this shit!" Without a second's notice, my back was being slammed onto the dock once again. I lost my breath on account of the pain. I hadn't even had a chance to heal from yesterday's injuries.

"Get your hands off my brother!" I heard Herman shout as the crowd began to turn into an angry mob of fists and fury. The large man took a fist to my jaw. I couldn't even process the pain. I was too busy thinking of how I had failed. I was out of a job once again. At that moment, I knew that my life could never be what I had hoped. There was no way Opal's family would willingly let her break off an engagement for a man who lived thousands of miles away and couldn't even sustain a job. It was over. I couldn't even bother to fight back. I was tired. I was so very, very tired.

"CUT IT OUT!" a low voice bellowed. It was so booming and authoritative. I felt the raucous of the entire raging mob fall to a hush all at once. Seconds later, the man who had pinned me down was being hoisted off of me with one fluid motion, like he was merely a sack of potatoes. To my surprise and confusion, Chip stood over me, huffing in air as his eyes burned into mine. The men remained silent as they watched to see what would come from this moment.

After what felt like days, without a word, Chip offered his hand to mine. Feeling empty of a fight, I took it, and he pulled me to my feet. Without letting go of my grip, he shook my hand firmly and then turned to acknowledge the workers.

"This man fights harder than any of you cowards here! I've never seen any of you girls ready to die for a cause like this man is." Stillness settled over the once unruly crowd. Not a word was whispered among them.

"It's time we gave this man the respect he has rightfully earned," Chip went on. "He's right. If Ranger did this to me, he would turn around and do it to every last one of ya. So, I will be the first to own my fault in not hearing him out sooner," Chip said, patting my back.

"C'mon now, Chip. He's tryin' to take money from our check! That really what you want?" a man from Chip's crew objected.

"Anybody confident enough in Ranger's winning personality and overall goodwill? Feel free to leave and go on about your business! Go on. I ain't gon' stop you!" Chip bellowed, losing his patience. "But before you do, why don't you take a good look at where that got me." To this, the objecting man fell silent. "Henry," Chip said, turning to me once again. "I'd like to hear what you have to say. Anybody have any objections to hearin' what this man's got to say?" Chip threatened. The crowd was silent. "Floor's all yours," he said, still maintaining his firm expression.

"Thank you, Chip," I replied, still floored by his sudden demonstration of good faith. "Gentlemen," I began again. "If we want a change, then we're gonna have to force a change!"

Chapter Twenty-three

Opal

St. Louis, MO
October 28, 1929

My dear sweet Henry,

Things are changing quickly here at home. I wish I could tell you everything, but, my dear, it is just too much to write. So, for now, I will simply tell you that I love you and that I hope to see you very soon. My love, I hope you haven't given up on me just yet. I hope you are still waiting for me and saving up enough for me to catch a train down to California to be with you. I am ready to be your wife, Henry. Write back to me soon.

With love,

Opal

As I sat at the vanity inside my bedroom, my words struck fear into my heart. I sealed up the letter and enclosed it in an envelope.

"I've called the Reverend over for lunch this afternoon," Mama said, poking her head into my room with a disapproving look on her face. "Perhaps he can talk some sense into you, child," she said behind a displeased tone. With a final look of disappointment, she disappeared from my doorway.

I took in a shaky breath of air and tucked the sealed envelope into a drawer beneath the mirror. I attempted to brush my hair but could not steady my trembling hand. I knew in my heart that I was right. But Mama had always ruled over my decisions. "Stay firm," I whispered to myself just as two more headaches waltzed into my room.

"Opal!" Nettie sang, dragging out my name as the pair pranced in. "Sounds like you're in trouble," Nettie teased as she and Hettie made themselves comfortable on my bed. I rolled my eyes at them and continued to brush my hair.

"Opal, are you ill or somethin'?" Hettie asked with genuine curiosity.

"No," I replied, shooting her a look through the mirror. "Why on earth would you ask that?"

"I heard Mama tell the Reverend that your head is filled with delusions. Does that mean you're sick?"

I slammed the brush down hard onto the table, startling both of the girls.

"Alright, that's enough, girls. Please leave," I yelled, shooing them out of my room and closing the door behind them.

I went to my bed and sat at the edge of it, sighing in despair. My breaths became shallow as I tried to inhale as many short breaths as I could. Try as I might, the panic had set in, and I couldn't seem to catch more than a breath or two. Tears betrayed my face as I hiccupped in short puffs of air. I lay across my bed and curled into a ball.

The more I thought about what I was doing, the more I wondered if I really was the fool that everyone assumed I was. In all my life, there hadn't ever been a feeling more lonely and more empty than this moment right now.

"Opal," I heard Mama's voice whisper. My eyes blinked wide open, and I realized that I had fallen asleep. Mama was brushing the stray hairs away from my face and smiling. "You really are such a stubborn girl," she said with a laugh as she looked over me with kind eyes. "It's time to get up now. The Reverend is downstairs and eager to speak with you."

Mama gave me one final glance and then quickly marched out of my room without another word. I rose from the comfort of my bed and made my way downstairs after Mama.

"I don't want to talk about this for too long as I have already made my decision," I said as we all began to cut into the chicken Mama had prepared. "I've got to run an errand in town later anyway."

Reverend Stone nodded and wiped his mouth with his napkin. "Of course. No use in dragging this out," he said with a kind smile. "Tell me, Opal. Why the sudden change?"

"Well, I don't suppose it was really as sudden a change as it appears to be," I said with a shrug.

"Is that right?" Reverend Stone replied, intrigued. "Why don't you tell me about that?"

I thought carefully about how I should answer. If I told the Reverend that I was secretly writing to Henry the entire time, then he would argue that I hadn't really given Thomas a fair chance. If I told him what Laura and I saw behind the alley trash cans just two days prior, it could ruin Thomas' reputation in St. Louis.

"Thomas and I could never have loved each other," I said, praying that was enough.

"Well, I think that's where you're wrong. I've officiated my fair share of weddings with couples that didn't have a spark in the beginning. But sooner or later, without any prompting on my or their parents' parts, the love always finds its way to them. Naturally."

"I don't think it would have come so naturally to Thomas," I said with a sigh. The Reverend cocked his head to one side, curious about my telling response. I noticed his left eyebrow twitched a little as he pondered what I meant. I quickly caught myself and added, "O-or myself."

"Huh," Reverend Stone said, with growing suspicion as he rubbed his chin.

Without warning, a memory sparked inside me. Suddenly it was yesterday, and I was back at Thomas' office, watching him rub his chin the exact same way, eyes focused on a patient's chart.

"Opal!" Thomas said, looking up from piles of papers scattered across his desk. He was clearly surprised to see me. "I thought you had plans with your family today. What are you doing here?"

"I-I needed to see you," I said with fear shooting through my veins.

"Oh? Is something the matter?" Thomas asked with concern, rising from his desk.

"No, no, not at all," I lied. "Well, no. That's not exactly true." Thomas approached me with worry in his eyes.

"What's the matter, dear? Did something happen with your mother?" Thomas caressed my face with a gentle palm.

"No, she's fine. I can assure you."

"Then what is it? Tell me, dear. You're shaking." Thomas said, escorting me in and shutting his office door behind us.

"I-I." I looked into his eyes as my stomach began to twist itself into tiny knots. "I can't marry you," I said, closing my eyes. Thomas' hands quickly left my cheek as his expression soured.

"Oh," he moaned, turning his back toward me. Guilt quickly set in, and I was unsure of how to continue. "That's not exactly the kind of news I'd hoped for," he said, with an embarrassed chuckle, squeezing the bridge of his nose. "Opal, I uh-" He paused to think. "I thought we had put all the back-and-forth nonsense behind us. Is this because of the travel abroad discussion we had yesterday?"

I shook my head quickly. "No, I think it's wonderful that you'd want to spend your days helping others."

"Well then, Jesus, Opal. What is it?" Thomas snapped, turning back toward me as he began to lose his patience. "I mean, I-I gave you space in the beginning when you were still getting over Henry. I didn't run for the hills. I likely should have, when you took months to give me an answer to my proposal. Y-you can't do this to me again! I gave you-"

"I saw you in the alley with Chester yesterday," I finally blurted out. Thomas fell silent, a look of horror quickly replacing his annoyed facial expression.

"Marriage is about time," Reverend Stone said, pulling me out of my daydream. "You're not supposed to have all the answers come wedding day. Each day is going to be a journey into learning the other person."

"I can't do that, not with Thomas," I replied.

"Why not, Opal?" the Reverend challenged. I noticed the Reverend's eyebrow had once again returned to the subtle twitch I had seen before. He continued to press me for answers. "Why not take a leap of faith? I know that it can be overwhelming, but succumbing to your fears is not the right answer."

"I love someone else. Henry Viefhaus," I said with fiery confidence that had somehow bubbled its way to the surface.

"Oh, for heaven's sake, Opal, not this again!" Mama huffed, rolling her eyes and slamming her napkin down on the table. "You haven't spoken to Henry in over two years! That can't possibly still be holding you back."

"That's exactly what's holding me back!" I yelled, stepping into my newfound courage more boldly now. "For the past ten months, I've been receiving letters from Henry while he's been in California." Mama's facial expression soured, and she was seconds away from throwing a complete fit.

"Mrs. Pleasant, please," Reverend Stone interjected. "I'd like to hear Opal out. Please, go on."

"What exactly do you think you saw?" I heard Thomas say as I found myself floating back into my memories from just yesterday. Thomas had a stone expression, and I could not tell what he was thinking.

"I-I saw the two of you holding hands, and you were laughing." Thomas folded his arms, not ready to hear me go on. "He kissed you. He kissed you twice," I cried. Thomas' eyes closed, and he let out a sigh of panic as he scratched his head. "Try as I might to be shocked," I went on, "or confused, angry, disappointed, or any emotion really," I said with a shrug, "I thought it all to be, well, very sad." Thomas' eyes darted to mine, and it was like we were finally on the same page, like we had finally made a connection. "I strangely found myself… somewhat envious. I suppose," I admitted as Thomas' anxious eyes burned a hole through my forehead. "I think we both know the two of us can't possibly go through with this marriage now."

"That's easy for you to say," Thomas finally said. "You can call off our marriage and go be with the one you love. No one will even give my love a second look."

"We may be fighting different battles, Thomas, but we both still bleed all the same," I argued.

"There is no battle, Opal! If you choose to be with Henry, you will be leaving me without a chance. The world will eat me alive and never think twice. You are my chance at normalcy."

"You can't actually expect me to go along with that, can you? To be your wife in name only? Never loving you, never having you love me? Could you honestly go through with something like this?" I asked, completely blindsided.

"When you're like me, you do what you have to do to survive," he said coldly.

"I can't do that. I'm sorry, Thomas. I-I'm so sorry, but I can't be your mask. I wish you well," I said, gathering my coat through shed tears and trotting towards his office door.

"No, you can't leave!" Thomas said, gripping my wrist. Before I knew it, he had spun behind me and blocked the only exit. "I won't let you leave," he declared, this time with more possession.

"Thomas," I said with a fear I had never felt around him before, "let me by."

"No." His eyes stared deep into mine, and I knew he wasn't thinking rationally anymore. "I am going to be your husband, and you will be my wife. I am the man, and we will do what I say is best!" His grip around my wrist grew tighter.

"Thomas, please, you're hurting me!"

"I will not be disrespected any longer!" he yelled into my face. "Not by you, not by my father, not by my professors, not by anyone!" I flinched but tried hard not to give away the panic I was feeling. Rage and fury were written in the lines on Thomas' tired face. I realized then that the only way I was getting out of his office was if I fought my way out. I suddenly had a flash of Mama's words she had once said to me years ago when I became of age. *A desperate man is a dangerous man.* Those words never seemed more true than in this moment.

I subtly scanned the office for anything heavy or sharp that I could use to temporarily disable Thomas long enough for me to escape. There was nothing.

"Thomas," I calmly tried again. "Please, let me by." He said nothing, only squeezed my wrist tighter. The pain was so sharp that my only instinct was to inflict immediate pain. Without a second thought, I found my knee involuntarily meeting with Thomas' groin. It worked. Thomas yelled out in what must have been excruciating pain. I took my chance and bolted for the door.

"Opal, please! I beg you to stay!" Thomas cried out from behind me. But I couldn't look back. The fear I felt was too great.

"You'll have to do this without me, Thomas. I'm sorry! I'm so sorry!" I sobbed.

"Henry has asked for my hand in marriage," I said to Mama and the Reverend, trying hard to push my daydreams out of my head once again. Mama gave the Reverend a pleading look. The Reverend gestured to her to remain calm. "I am going to California to accept his proposal," I said with confidence. At this, Mama rose from the table and stormed out of the dining room.

"Opal," the Reverend said with a look of curiosity. If I might ask, where did it all go wrong for you and Thomas? Last we spoke, you were as giddy as a schoolgirl, excited to plan a beautiful wedding," he said, as his left eyebrow once again began to twitch. I was quiet for a beat as I pondered his words.

"It could never have been real for Thomas and me. I think somewhere deep down, we both knew that."

"So, nothing's happened? No apparent issues you want to tell me about? I might be able to help you if you tell me," he said.

I suddenly wanted to believe that the Reverend had the best intentions. But for whatever reason, I couldn't seem to pry my focus away from his recurring twitch every time Thomas was mentioned. It seemed every time he inquired about Thomas, the twitch would start almost instantaneously. It gave me an uneasy feeling, like perhaps the Reverend had suspicions of his own, and I was going to be the girl who brought all the secrets to light. At that moment, I knew that, though I would never be with Thomas, I needed to protect him.

"Nothing," I said. "It was just not meant to be."

Chapter Twenty-four

Opal

"Honestly, Opal. Do you really think that there wouldn't be consequences to your actions?" Mama said angrily, following me around my room. The morning consisted of two hours of arguing and bickering over my decision to break things off with Thomas.

"Mama, please. I don't want to-"

"No, Opal! You need to give me a better reason than *it just didn't work*. We've all put a lot of effort into this, and I've had just about enough of your dramatics. Now you tell me what's going on this instant!"

"We didn't want to marry! That's all there is to it. Would you please stop pestering me on and on about this?" I said with more sass than intended. Mama's eyes widened.

"I've been taking care of you for eighteen years, Opal Pleasant. I won't tolerate disrespect, not now, not ever. You hear me?"

I nodded in agreement, even though my blood boiled within. "Mama, I don't know what else you want me to say," I said, offering a kinder tone. "Thomas and I have already decided to call things off."

"But why, child? Why this sudden change? Betrothals don't just end at the snap of a finger."

"Well, this one does," I replied, hoping she would just leave it at that.

"Then tell me why!"

"For heaven's sake, Mama! I can't!"

"Why not? Why can't you tell me what-"

Before Mama could even finish her next sentence, there was a nervous knock at my bedroom door. Nettie and Hettie stood in the doorway, eyes wide with concern.

"Out of here, girls," Mama said with a stern voice. "This is a private discussion."

"Opal has a visitor," Nettie said with a mousy tone.

"Who?" I asked. Before Nettie could reply, Thomas appeared in the doorway behind the girls, hat in hand.

"Thomas," I said, amazed by his timing, yet equally nervous about his presence, given our last encounter. "Never thought I'd be seeing you here again, especially so soon after everything. Is something the matter?"

"I needed to speak with you," Thomas said, stepping into my room. "I hope that's alright."

I looked over at Mama, and she quickly excused herself, shooing the girls out with her as she closed the door behind herself. I knew deep down she was hoping that Thomas was here to make things right and reconcile everything that had brought us to this very point. Had she only known the truth, she'd know there was no turning back.

"What is it?" I asked with a guarded tone. "If you're here to try and force me to pretend to be your wife, the answer is still no. I-I want to protect you, but this isn't the way to-"

"I spoke to Reverend Stone yesterday," he cut in. "He told me the two of you discussed the decision to call off the wedding."

"Oh," I said, wondering where his thoughts were leading him.

"I wanted to thank you, Opal."

"Thank me?"

"When I heard the two of you had met to discuss things," he shook his head in wonder, "I thought surely my reputation was ruined forever, especially after the horrible way I'd acted. I thought you'd have no reason to protect my shameful secret." I stood silently as he spoke. "I-I'm terribly sorry, Opal. I hope you can find it in your heart to forgive me someday."

"You're not shameful, Thomas," I said after some thought. "You're a good man. I've always known that. It's why I agreed to marry you before, even though my heart belonged to another."

Thomas squeezed my hand and nodded. "And you're the most compassionate woman I've ever met," he declared. "I won't stand in your way any longer. You should go and be with Henry."

"I wish you nothing but happiness," I whispered, giving his hand a genuine squeeze in return. Thomas nodded in agreement.

"I've decided to go with Chester to Sudan. We're going to give medical care to those without it. It won't be complete freedom, but at least we'll be together."

We were both quiet for a moment. Then silently, Thomas kissed my cheek and dismissed himself. "I wish you well, Opal." With those words, he vanished.

Just moments after, I heard the front door to our house close. Mama walked in, right on cue. I rolled my eyes and sighed obnoxiously as I sat on the bed, preparing for the second half of our argument.

I reached into my apron pocket and revealed the diamond ring that Henry had sent me and held it up for Mama to see. "Henry sent this to me," I said with a pause. I watched her eyes go wide and then slowly tighten as she struggled to fight her own disappointment. "Before you go on griping and complaining about all this, I just need you to know Mama that it's over between Thomas and me. I'm going to California. I've made up my mind, and this time no one is going to stop me. I was honestly hoping that you'd be my first supporter in all this."

Mama let out a sigh and exited the room. At that moment, I was sure she'd never forgive me. But to my surprise, just moments later, she reappeared with a necklace in her right hand and a folded piece of paper in the other. She handed the paper to me first.

"Open it," she said. I quickly obeyed and found a short note written inside.

You always make your own decisions. That's why I'm so proud of you.

Love,

Daddy

"Where did you get this?" I asked Mama through sudden blinding tears.

"Your father wrote that when you were just five years old. It was right after you told him that you hated pinto beans and demanded that we only give you potatoes for dinner." Mama laughed to herself, and it made me smile. She handed me the necklace in her hand. "You've always been stubborn and painfully independent," she said with a loving tone. "When you and Thomas were first engaged, I sent word down to your father's last remaining kin in Tennessee, begging them to send me this."

Mama handed me the necklace. It was a simple thin gold chain with a pearly white stone dangling at the center.

"We named you Opal after your grandmother's birthstone. This necklace was hers. Your father and I decided we would give it to you when we felt you had finally become a woman. I was preparing to give it to you on your wedding day with Thomas. I can see now that you're more of a woman now than I realized."

"Thank you, Mama," I said, turning so she could place the necklace around my neck.

"I won't fight you anymore, girl," Mama chuckled. "You are as strong as an ox, and I know my days of worrying over you are coming to an end."

I quickly rose to hug her, touched that she could finally see me as an adult, as a woman.

"Look at me, Opal," Mama said, clasping her soft palm against my chin. She stared at me for a long while, finally breaking her silence with a kiss to my forehead. “You have my blessing.”

Chapter Twenty-five

Henry

A knock at the door brought me out of the storm of papers that flood my desk. I scratched my head before yelling for the visitor to enter.

"Henry?" a sweet voice said. I looked up to see Cathy's bright smile in the doorway.

"Cathy!" I yelled, rising from my desk. "What a pleasant surprise. You look positively radiant!"

"Me? What about you, Mister Longshoreman Director?" she said, giggling into her hand as she embraced me.

I laughed nervously, feeling sudden guilt in her presence. "I suppose. It's only been a week, but I have absolutely no idea how to run this place."

"Oh, nonsense," she said, waving off my comment. "If anyone can run this place, it's you!"

"Please, sit," I said, motioning to the chair across from mine at my desk. We both took our seats quickly, though the awkwardness lingered like a dark cloud above us. She stared at me blankly for a moment. I couldn't bare the silence.

"Cathy, I uh-" I began, "I hope there aren't any hard feelings with your father about all this. Mr. Ranger was an incredible director, and I'm sure I'll learn very quickly how much it takes to keep a place like this running."

"Oh, stop it!" Cathy said with a shake of her head. "I came down here to thank you! Had it not been for you and your friends protesting, the board of directors might have never known how bad things were here. Besides, doctors have been tellin' my daddy for years that the stress from this place was hard on his heart. If they hadn't forced him to resign, he would've never left!" she said with a laugh.

I laughed as well, still a tad guarded, knowing that I was the reason her dad lost his job.

"So, you gonna start that union, like you've been planning?" Cathy asked.

"That's the goal," I said with a nod. "There's still a lot that must be done to make it happen, but I intend to fight for it tooth and nail." Cathy nodded but said nothing. I felt a slight awkwardness fill the space between us as I searched for what to say next.

"I still feel terrible about your father," I said humbly. "What will your family do now?"

"Don't you worry about us, Henry!" Cathy said, waving off my concerns. "We'll do just fine. Daddy's still got his pension. Jacob and I plan on pitching in as much as we can, just as soon as we're married."

"Oh, so there's going to be a wedding?" I said, perking up.

"Oh, yes! Daddy's already agreed to help us buy a home."

"Wow, glad to see he's had such a change of heart."

"If it wasn't for you, Henry," Cathy said, shaking her head. "I'm so grateful for your friendship. In fact, that's why I wanted to come by today. It seems I need your help once again."

"Of course!" I said, eager to make things right. "Whatever you need, I'm there."

"Well, I know Jacob would just have a fit if he knew I was here on his behalf, but if we're to be married soon, we'd have to have a stable income."

"I see."

"Now that you're the longshoreman director, I was hoping that you might have something for him here on the docks."

"Consider it done," I said with a smile. "Can he start tomorrow?"

"Oh, Henry!" Cathy beamed. "I don't know how I can ever repay you!" She stood up at once and clasped her hands together. "You are a godsend, Henry Viefhaus."

I stood as well and escorted her toward the door, confident that I could tackle any problem that came walking through those office doors.

"Of course, Cathy," I replied. "I hope you will always count me as a friend." She nodded and skipped out of my office.

"Of course, dear!" her voice called. "Jacob will be absolutely thrilled!"

No sooner had Cathy turned the corner and pranced down the hall did another familiar face appear.

"Hello, Henry," she said with a bashful smirk.

"Dottie," I said, my surprise less than subtle. "H-How are you?"

"Better," she said, rubbing her stomach. "Much better than the last time we spoke. I heard about the protest. It takes an amazing man to pull something like that off."

I nodded without a word. I started to speak, but before I could, Dottie cut in.

"I believe I owe you an apology for last week. I was in a crisis, and I was scared. I wanted you to come in and fix it all for me. I wanted you to be my personal knight in shining armor. I can see now how selfish that was."

"Dottie," I began, "there's no need to-"

"Please, let me finish." She put a hand up to silence me. "I'm afraid if I don't, I'll never say what it is I need to say." She gave a nervous laugh as I nodded in agreement.

"Well then, no need to speak so vulnerably in the halls. Please, come in," I said.

"That's alright. I actually have a bus to catch to the Union Station. I can't be too long."

"Union Station?" I asked. "Where are you going?"

"Henry dear, please," she said through shaky breaths. "I only wanted to thank you for your patience with me. Your friendship has made such an impact on me." I nodded, forcing myself not to pry but wanting an answer to what was going on. "I don't know whether my feelings toward you could ever completely vanish," she said, eyes glued to the floor. "Knowing that we'll always remain friends, brings a certain comfort to me now."

"Thank you for saying that, Dottie," I said after a pause. "The last thing I want is for our friendship to end. I hope you can see that still."

"Oh, Henry," Dottie said, patting my shoulder. "You've always had the best intentions… I know that for a fact."

"May I ask why you're on your way to the Union Station?" I said, eyebrows raised.

"You sly dog. You just have to know it all, don't you?" Dottie said with a more comfortable giggle. We both shared a laugh, and for the first time in a long time, it felt like we were us again. "Well, if you must know, Jeffrey and I are headed North to San Francisco. I told him if we were going to marry, I'd have to have my mama and daddy present. No exceptions."

"Marry?" I said, a little surprised. "You're still going through with that?"

"Well, Henry, what's a girl to do?" Dottie chuckled with a slightly more serious expression. "I can't exactly raise the baby alone, can I?"

"What happened to the fiery, independent Dottie that would never let a man tie her down?" I asked jokingly.

"Things change," she shrugged after mild consideration. "It's time for me to grow up and take some responsibility I guess." We both stood there staring at each other, likely both wondering how in the world we ended up here, at this exact moment. "Besides," she continued, "I've got more of a soft spot for Jeffrey than you might think." She winked at me, and I smiled back at her with ease.

"Is that so?" I asked, intrigued. "Is someone developing a little crush?"

"Mr. Viefhaus," Dottie giggled, "now you know I am not one to kiss and tell, so you may as well erase your suspicions now!"

"Alright, alright," I said, putting my hands up in surrender. We sat in silence for a while before I continued. "Dottie, I uh… I hope you'll always know how much you mean to me," I said, scratching the back of my head. "You were there when no one else could understand. I am forever grateful for that."

"Oh, Henry dear," she replied sweetly, "you are a breath of fresh air in this California heat. Thanks for always being a safe place for me too." Dottie reached into her purse as she spoke and revealed a pocket watch. She quickly read the time and replaced the item back into her purse. "I'd best get goin'," she said. "I'll be home after New Year's. Hopefully, we'll both be newlyweds by then?" she asked with eyebrows raised. I chuckled and nodded in agreement.

"Yes," I replied. "I am most definitely counting on it."

Chapter Twenty-six

Opal

San Pedro CA
November 3, 1929

Hello Honey,

How's St. Louis? Well, dear, it is true that time has told all. It has proven our love everlasting and also is now driving us closer and closer. How happy I shall be when time has driven us, not only closer but together as I have so long dreamed. Then, dear, you will find not only that my love has never faltered, but you will find me one of the happiest men that you have ever seen.

Sweetheart, I'm counting the days until you are pronounced mine. Opal dear, never let the ideas of other people have any influence on you or your plans for the future. For dear, if you are so brave and so sweet as to come here, all this distance, to be happy and to make me happy, you are to be loved and envied and not censored. For honey, if you are ready and willing to take me, as I'm so anxious to take you, then we should not be kept apart when we are so in love and never by what some may think. I am hoping that your dear mother will not object to your coming to me, for dear, I can't do without you much longer.

Honey babe, I'm already so darn happy that I could just shout for joy to think and to know that within weeks from the date that is stamped on this letter, you could be here in my arms, my life, and my little world of happiness. Just think, dear, what that means to me, what you mean to me. This will be the realization of a dream that I silently dreamed and planned several, long years ago when I met you in Mr. Penny's shoe store. You never knew it but even when I first met you, I often thought what a wonderful wife you would make for some man. I even discussed your wonderful qualities with my brother, Herman, and he has always wished me success in winning you.

And now, dear one, that we are so near, he will be pleased to know that we are going to be married. But happy, say, I'm the boy who will be happy, and my greatest happiness will be in making you happy, Opal dear. Of course, you are aware that you are going to marry only a man with a fairly good job, a healthy body and a heart that beats for you. And when you are here, I will have a short vacation and then we will settle down to the life that appeals to me, the life of a happily-married, young couple, and try to live life as it comes and as we see best fit.

I'm so sorry, Opal, that I cannot give you the luxury that you really deserve, as I wish I could, and have entertained hopes of doing. But Opal, if you can be satisfied with my love and my ability to make us a livelihood and home, then you are the one for me. Honey when that train rolls into Los Angeles with you aboard, then happiness is rolling to me, for you are the only one who can bring me the happiness that I've so often dreamed of. Honey, I hope your friends are not so very lonesome for you when you are gone, but I'm sure they will miss such a sweet thing as you. But their lonesomeness cannot come to compare with the lonely hours I've waited for you, for two years.

Dear, on your next opportunity, go to the station and ask if the train schedule from St. Louis to L.A. is as I've said and about not having to change cars, etc. Learn all the particulars regarding your trip and get your ticket in advance so you will have a good berth reserved. Then send me an airmail letter or telegram and name definitely the date and hour of your departure there and your arrival here. For I can't fail to meet that train. But I won't. I'll be right there with waiting. Waiting for my first, my only and my everlasting love and sweetheart, to take her home and into my life and future as the sweetest of the whole creation of God's loveliest. Dearest, I'm making this a rather long letter, but dear I love you. I'm happy and content when I can sit down and write to the sweetest girl on earth, to you.

I have enclosed a money order for one hundred and fifty dollars. Please write me when you receive it, so I can know that my darling girl is in route to me. And with a blessing and prayer, I know it will bring you to me safely. Now, Opal, I will closely wait for another sweet letter from you and continue thinking of you and the happy hours to come.

Sincerest of love, your own,

Henry

Extend my sincerest regard to your mother.

"Look at my baby girl, all grown up," Mama said, dabbing at her eyes as the attendant at the window handed me a boarding pass. "Where has the time gone?" she asked with a bittersweet smile.

I thanked the attendant, gripping the handle on my duffle bag a little tighter, nerves overtaking my every breath. Loud train whistles could be heard from the other end of the Union Station, and they made my stomach flutter.

"Don't fret, Opal. It's all going to turn out great!" Laura declared. She had practically begged to accompany Mama and the twins in escorting me off to California. I nodded at her and took a deep breath, knowing she was right.

Mama and the twins wore their Sunday best to the station. Mama didn't think it'd be appropriate to come in her everyday clothes. She was even wearing lipstick and rouge. Mama continued to dab her eyes every chance she got and was an emotional wreck. Although, I can't say leaving was any easier on me. I found my eyes welling with each passing moment, and a part of me didn't see how I could ever leave my family behind to start my new life with Henry.

Another train whistle blew in the distance. We all turned to see steam coming out of the smokestack of a train nearby. Seconds later, an older gentleman wearing a station uniform appeared from one of the train cars.

"Now boarding for *Train 451*, first call!" he called out loudly. "Now boarding for *Train 451*, St. Louis to Los Angeles, first call!" he yelled again.

Butterflies seemed to swarm within me when I heard it. Within seconds, people were lining up single-file to hand him their tickets as they boarded.

"Looks like that's you, Opal!" Nettie said, with an eager smile on her face. I don't think it had fully registered to her that I would not be seeing her for some time. My eyes welled up just thinking about it.

I gripped my duffle bag and took in a deep breath.

"I suppose it is," I said calmly.

"Oh, Opal!" Mama said, squeezing me tightly at the shoulders. "I'm going to be absolutely miserable without you," she declared, pulling out her handkerchief and dabbing once again. "Does Henry have a telephone that you can use when you arrive there? I won't be able to wait for a letter. I'll be too anxious."

"I don't know, Mama. But I promise to ask as soon as I arrive," I replied.

"Well, even if he doesn't," she said, shaking her head, "you ask him to take you somewhere that does, and you call the post office and have Leroy take a message. I'm in town enough to stop by there and make sure you've made it safely.

Just as Mama said this, it hit me. "The letter," I said, eyes wide.

"Letter? What letter?" Mama asked.

"The one I wrote to Henry last night. I meant to drop it by the post office before we arrived, and it completely slipped my mind!" I said, frantically searching through my duffle bag for it.

"Second call! Second call for *Train 451*!" I heard the uniformed man call out.

"Well, what's the difference now, dear? You'll be seeing him in just a few days," Mama asked. I said nothing and continued to search for it.

"Second call for *Train 451*, St. Louis to Los Angeles!" the man yelled out again.

"Well don't dawdle, Opal," Mama said, getting flustered. "You don't want to miss your train over some silly letter!"

"Yes, but I wanted to let Henry know that everything has gone over as planned, and I'm in route," I said, finally retrieving the letter from my bag and holding it in the air as if it were some sort of trophy.

"You don't have time to run back now, Opal," Laura said with concern.

"Last call!" The man called out. "Last and final call for *Train 451*!"

I looked back at the train with dread, fearing that without my final letter, Henry wouldn't know that I was on the way to him.

"I can take it for you," Laura said, extending out a hand.

"Oh, Laura, are you sure?" I said, with pleading eyes.

"It's no trouble at all." She gave me a friendly smile.

"Well, it's just that the first letters go out this morning at ten o'clock. My letter has to beat me to Los Angeles, so it has to be in that shipment," I said, pointing to the large clock that hung overhead a large hallway in the station. The clock read nine-forty.

"Well then, we've got no time to lose!" Laura said, extending her hand out a final time.

"Last and final call for *Train 451*!" the man called again.

"And it looks like, neither do you," Laura chuckled. I handed her the letter, and she embraced me tightly. "Promise you'll write to me?" she said pulling away and swiping a stray tear from her cheek. I nodded in agreement.

"I promise," I replied. Without another word, Laura went dashing down the large hall with the clock hung above it and disappeared.

"Last caaaaall!" The man dragged out the word, and I knew before long they'd be shutting the doors for good.

"We'll miss you, Opal!" Hettie said, as she quickly wrapped her arms around my waist. Nettie joined her, and they both held on real tight.

Mama smiled as she watched us, and I could tell that this would be the hardest on her. After the twins let go, Mama hugged me and pecked my cheek.

"You're such a good girl," she said. "You're going to be just fine out there on your own." I nodded back and kissed her cheek, feeling as ready as I'd ever been to board. I gave my family one final look. They were beautiful. I was proud that they were mine.

Without another minute to spare, I quickly skipped over to the attending man and handed him my boarding pass. He punched a hole through the corner of it and smiled, handing it back to me.

"Enjoy your ride, Miss," he said. I nodded with a smile as I boarded the train.

Once in my seat, I glanced out the window to see Mama and the girls, waiting for me to take off. The twins waved uncontrollably with cheerful expressions on their faces. I smiled and gave them a wave in return. Mama just looked on and smiled, trying her best not to cry.

"All aboard!" I hear the man's voice call out. "Aaaaall aboard!" he dragged his voice out again. Suddenly, there was a loud sound of steam being released. The train began to rock as we slowly moved forward.

Mama and the girls continued to watch, waiting until I was completely out of sight. I waved and waved until they were all but specks in my rearview. I could feel myself already missing them. I was suddenly overwhelmed with emotion and allowed myself to cry a little.

A mother sitting across from me, trying her best to calm a toddler and an infant, silently reached into her purse and handed me her handkerchief. I nodded a silent thank you and consoled myself.

After a few minutes had passed, we were no longer in the city. I could see plains that seemed to stretch on for miles. I don't know how I had lived in St. Louis for all this time and never saw such beauty. It made me happy. I suddenly felt calm.

I thought about what Henry must be doing at this exact moment. Was he waiting for me? Doing his best to prepare our future home together? Perhaps he was on the docks this very moment, trying to make a living for our little family. Excitement suddenly overcame me. Before that moment, I never knew so surely just how right I was about my life. How right I was about Henry.

Chapter Twenty-seven

The Last Letter
Opal

St. Louis, MO
November 8, 1929

Henry Dear,

Your very sweet letter came today. I am so full of joy to know that finally, after two years of waiting, we can be together. Yes, dear, I suppose my friends will miss me. But I know they will soon be happy knowing that I am with my husband and starting a life with you. You haven't seen me for a long, long time. But if you are real sure that you want me, I am sure that I want you.

And dear, don't worry yourself about Mama. I have seen a change in her. She has made it clear that if I want to go, then she will not stop me from doing so.

Oh, darling, I can only imagine what you must have gone through to afford sending for me to come to California. Just know that your efforts have not gone unnoticed, dear one.

I cannot wait to be with you, the one I am willing to take for richer or poorer, better or worse, and to love and follow to the end of my life. It is going to be a wonderful life. I am so honored to have the privilege of soon being called your wife.

I am going to love you always, Henry, my dear one. And honey, just know that what you can't give me, I don't want. And the one thing you can give me is love, and that I feel sure that you will give. And dear, I am sure that you are not the only one that will be happy when I arrive, so darling, I pray that this letter will get to you quickly, for I am finally coming to California! I should arrive on November 11th, late in the evening.

So bye-bye, for now, darling, and I will see you real soon. I am counting the hours until I get to be with you. So wait patiently, and it won't be so long.

Love,

Your Opal.

P.S. I have received the money.